How Donald Trump Won the 2016 Presidential Election and Disarrayed the Political Establishment

Janvier T. Chando

TISI BOOKS

NEW YORK, RALEIGH, LONDON, AMSTERDAM

PUBLISHED BY TISI BOOKS
www.tisibooks.com

ISBN-13: 978-1-7180-4266-7
ISBN-10: 1-7180-4266-3

PUBLISHED BY TISI BOOKS
www.tisibooks.com

NEW YORK, RALEIGH, LONDON, AMSTERDAM

Printed in The United States of America

Titles by Janvier Chouteu-Chando

The Usurper: and Other Stories
Triple Agent, Double Cross
Disciples of Fortune
The Union Moujik
Splendid Comets
Flash of the Sun
Fortune Calls
Fortune's Master
Fortune's Children
The Norilsk Bears
To Be In Love and To Be Wise
The Fire and Ice Legend
The Sweetest Madness
The Grandmothers
The Hunger Fire
The Shades of Fire
Father and Sons
The Doctors
Dark Shades
Fateful Ties
The Verdict of Hades
His Majesty's Trial
Ngoko's Folly
The Usurper
The Dowry
I am Hated
The Oaf

Non-Fiction Titles by Janvier Chouteu-Chando

FALLEN HEROES: African Leaders Whose Assassinations…
BROKEN ENGAGEMENT: Why a Donald Trump Win…
THEIR LAST STAND: Donald Trump's Upset Victory…
Ukraine: The Tug-of-war between Russia and the West
THE CANARY IN A COAL MINE EFFECT:…
Cameroon: The Haunted Heart of Africa

Quotes

If the freedom of speech is taken away then dumb and silent we may be led, like sheep to the slaughter.
George Washington

If Tyranny and Oppression come to this land, it will be in the guise of fighting a foreign enemy.
James Madison

I hold it, that a little rebellion, now and then, is a good thing, and as necessary in the political world as storms in the physical.
Thomas Jefferson

Remember, democracy never lasts long. It soon wastes, exhausts, and murders itself. There never was a democracy yet that did not commit suicide.
John Adams

The best form of government is that which is most likely to prevent the greatest sum of evil.
James Monroe

Contents

Quotes	5
Dedication	9
Maps	11
Chapter 1: *Forewarnings*	15
Chapter 2: *Ethnicity*	36
Chapter 3: *Immigration*	57
Chapter 4: *Electoral College/Popular Vote Disconnect*	75
Chapter 5: *Economy & Declining Income*	93
Chapter 6: *Religion*	113
Chapter 7: *Globalization and States that Lost Jobs from it*	129
Chapter 8: *Dissatisfaction with the Choice of Candidates*	142
Chapter 9: *Clearness of the Message and Campaign Slogans*	144
Chapter 10: *Turnout*	146
Chapter 11: *Rural voters*	151
Chapter 12: *The Size of the Campaign Area*	156
Chapter 13: *Education*	160
Chapter 14: *The Media and the Democratic Nominee*	167

DEDICATION

This book is for the United States of America that cannot be deprived of its fine tomorrow, and is also for the world that refuses to be plunged into darkness.

More especially, it is for Man in the post-modernist world as we try to make sense of reality not only as Humans who are in sync with their surroundings but also as beings who accept their purpose on this earth.

This account is also dedicated to the people and countries in the Middle-East, Asia, and Africa that are humane and that are suffering from established dictatorships, overwhelming oppression and brutal repression, but who still view democracy, freedom, social justice, liberty, equality and progress as the tools that would prevent them from becoming dehumanized, and so are prepared to oppose their oppressors, especially in countries like Cameroon, Chad, Congo Gabon, Eritrea, Gambia, Democratic Republic of Congo and Zimbabwe.

Maps

Map of the USA

2008 Presidential Election Map

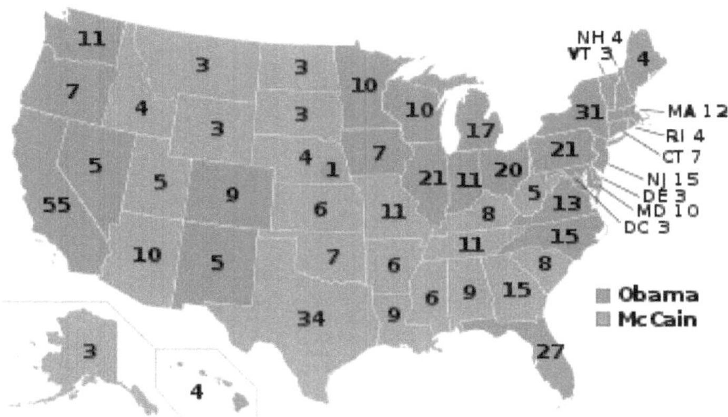

2012 Presidential Election Map

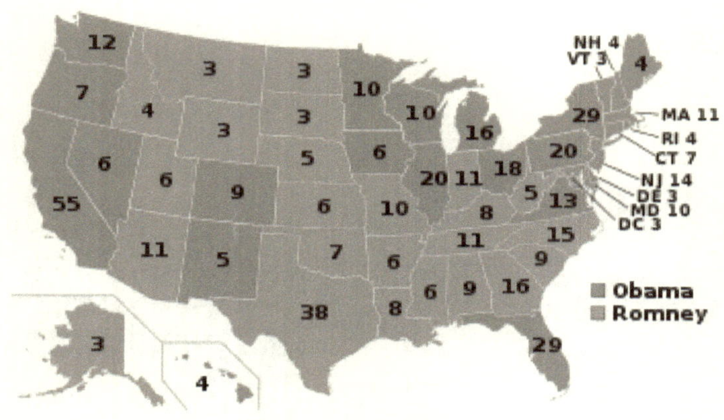

2016 Presidential Election Map

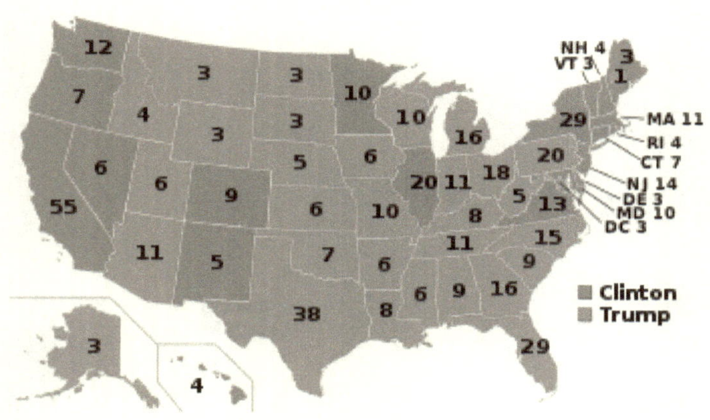

Summary of results of the 2004- 2016 Presidential Elections:

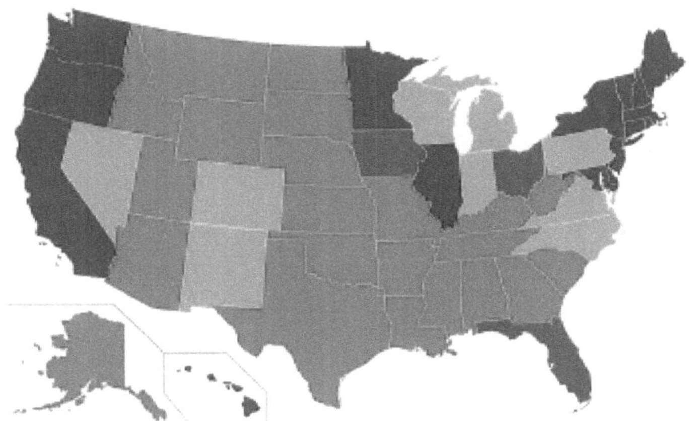

CHAPTER ONE

Forewarnings

The Clinton campaign should have heeded the alarm bells set off by the piece *5 Reasons Why Trump Will Win*, written before the election by the famous American documentary filmmaker and author Michael Francis Moore who rose to fame from his 2002 book *"Stupid White Men...and Other Sorry Excuses for the State of the Nation!"* and from his 2004 documentary film *"Fahrenheit 9/11"* that talked about the 43rd US. President George W. Bush, and the War on Terror. After all, he is a left-wing liberal. Even the other insightful piece *BROKEN ENGAGEMENT: Why a Donald Trump Win in the 2016 Presidential Election Defies the Predictions of the Media and the Political establishment*, should have been taken seriously as the final warning cry coming on the heels of a series of earlier pronouncements about the reasons why the Republican Presidential nominee Donald John Trump could win the 2016 race for the White House against Hillary Rodham Clinton of the Democratic Party.

Apparently, the anti-Trump campaign was oblivious of the warnings from these two unrelated pieces, which were certainly a few of the many similar predictions out there defying the popular forecasts from the mainstream media and polling agencies showing

Hillary Clinton as the candidate ahead in the polls and as the front-runner expected to win the 2016 race for the White House. But the results below show that it was not the case. The Republican Party nominee pulled off a dramatic upset over her Democratic Party rival in what many pundits, newsmen, newswomen, scholars, and pollsters consider to be the biggest electoral surprise in the history of Presidential Elections in the USA.

Results of the 2016 Presidential Election

Presidential candidate	Party	Popular Vote		Electoral vote
		Count	Percentage	
Donald Trump	Republican	62,853,327	46.09%	306
Hillary Clinton	Democratic	65,515,369	48.05%	232
Gary Johnson	Libertarian	4,478,969	3.28%	0
Jill Stein	Green	1,450,670	1.06%	0

Evan McMullin	Independent	*656,095*	*0.48%*	*0*
Darrell Castle	Constitution	*199,895*	*0.15%*	*0*
Other		*1,205,061*	*0.88%*	—
	Total	*136,359,386*	100%	*538*
	Needed to win			270

Months before the election and even right up to election day itself, Hillary Clinton led in almost every national poll in Florida, North Carolina, Michigan, Pennsylvania, Wisconsin. Yet, she ended up losing those states. In fact, the average absolute difference between polling average and final vote in the 10 states closest to the national average revealed that her poll results were off the final result by 3.9 points, the highest in any election since 1988. This is compared to 2.3 points in 2012, 1.7 points in 2008 and 2004, 1.9 points in 2000, 2.3 points in 1996, 3.4 points in 1992 and 1988.

Most Americans and the overwhelming majority of the citizens of other countries of the world are still reeling from the unexpected results, which hardly anyone would disagree turned out to be the most unpredictable, most abnormal and most unconventional race for the White House in the recent history of the United States of America.

No one can pretend that the shock victory of the Republican Party nominee, businessman and reality television star from New York Donald John Trump over Hillary Diane Rodham Clinton of the Democratic Party has not turned the evolutionary nature of American politics upside down. In fact, it has ushered into office a novice with no past political experience, with no clearly defined political ideology and with a history of unfriendly or hostile relations with most of the elites of both the Republican Party on whose ticket he rode to victory, and the Democratic Party that people still remember he was formerly a member of.

This most unconventional election in American history that defied the predictions of most political pundits, the mainstream the media and the general conventions, and then ended up bringing to power a maverick with a populist streak, will be remembered for generations as a "Go to Hell" expression from mostly White Americans, especially white men. It is a rebuff of the elites of both the Republican and Democratic parties who thrive in alliance with the giant corporations, the corporate or mainstream media, and the financial institutions (Wall Street, the banks, the insurance companies and the Credit companies). And strangely enough, Donald Trump, the poster child of this blunt rejection of the political establishment, happens to be a renegade child of the political establishment, which he worked with to build his business empire, and on which he created the base that he launched his political bid for the White House from. But then, he turned around and confronted them.

This renegade of the political establishment may be considered a peculiar president-elect whose vague agenda to turn the political establishment upside down and whose pledge to "Make America Great Again", smacks of Anarchism than conservatism or any of the other shades of Right-wing Republican ideology around which clear programs have been hatched in the past to right the shortcomings of the American system, a setup that for centuries proved to be the most progressive socio-economic/political system the world has ever seen, a system that has been the standard bearer of the free world, a system that stands to retain its emulative role if properly harnessed and revamped.

- How did Donald Trump, considered a political outsider by everyone, capture a political party whose leadership shunned him, and then lead it to win the White House in a race that was apparently unwinnable for him and the Republican Party whose ticket he was riding on?
- How come a maverick known for his non-affiliation with traditional politics, a maverick who is considered a political novice by most pundits and who has a knack for being politically incorrect by "saying things the way they really are", or the way he feels they are; how come this outsider who many people viewed as someone with a knack for being "brutally honest" managed to hold a great country like America in suspense, and then turned things around and won the race for the White House against all the odds?

Yes, the odds were stacked against Donald Trump, yet he prevailed. And he triumphed in a brilliant manner.

Stacked against the Republican candidate in the 2016 Presidential Election were:

- the no-nonsense Obama administration and its political machinery that won the 2008 and 2012 Presidential Elections with wide margins,
- the all-powerful mainstream media,
- an opponent with a formidable alliance centered

around the administration of Hillary Clinton's husband—the former president William Jefferson Clinton (Bill Clinton) and his retinue, all at the service of the Democratic candidate,

- the divided ranks of the upper echelons of the Republican Party, where most of the party's elites vehemently opposed the Republican nominee,

- what some viewed as a corporatocracy that did not consider the Republican nominee and billionaire as one of their own,

- a Wall Street and big financial institutions who were not enamored of him and whom he snubbed by not seeking their financial contributions to fund his election campaign,

- Hillary Clinton running as the first female presidential candidate in the history of the United States of America, hence a source of attraction for voters with a desire to make history with their votes.

So, why then did the election end up not being the walkover that so many pundits and even the common folk had predicted, and that the Democratic Party had promised; why then did the election fail to be the thrashing of Donald Trump that was supposed to silence the Republican candidate forever; why then was the election not an easy victory for Hillary Clinton, a stroll into the White House that would have made her the first female president in the history of the United States of America, and the first person in the country's history to hold the positions of president after making a name for herself in previous positions as the country's First Lady, as a senator and as America's secretary of state?

The answers were predictable to those with curious and analytical minds.

2016 Presidential Election Results by States

States won by Clinton/Kaine

States won by Trump/Pence

Electoral methods

- WTA – Winner-takes-all
- CD – Congressional district*

State or district	Electoral method	Hillary Clinton Democratic			Donald Trump Republican		
		#	%	Electoral votes	#	%	Electoral votes
Alabama	WTA	729,547	34.36	–	1,318,255	62.08	9
Alaska	WTA	116,454	36.55	–	163,387	51.28	3
Arizona	WTA	1,161,167	45.13	–	1,252,401	48.67	11

JANVIER T. CHANDO

State or district	Electoral method	Hillary Clinton Democratic			Donald Trump Republican		
		#	%	Electoral votes	#	%	Electoral votes
Arkansas	WTA	380,494	33.65	–	684,872	60.57	6
California	WTA	8,696,374	62.28	55	4,452,094	31.88	–
Colorado	WTA	1,338,870	48.16	9	1,202,484	43.25	–
Connecticut	WTA	897,572	54.57	7	673,215	40.93	–
Delaware	WTA	235,603	53.35	3	185,127	41.92	–
District of Columbia	WTA	282,830	90.48	3	12,723	4.07	–
Florida	WTA	4,504,975	47.82	–	4,617,886	49.02	29
Georgia	WTA	1,877,963	45.89	–	2,089,104	51.05	16
Hawaii	WTA	266,891	60.98	4	128,847	29.44	–

State or district	Electoral method	Hillary Clinton Democratic			Donald Trump Republican		
		#	%	Electoral votes	#	%	Electoral votes
Idaho	WTA	189,765	27.49	–	409,055	59.26	4
Illinois	WTA	3,090,729	55.83	20	2,146,015	38.76	–
Indiana	WTA	1,039,126	37.91	–	1,557,286	56.82	11
Iowa	WTA	653,669	41.74	–	800,983	51.15	6
Kansas	WTA	427,005	36.05	–	671,018	56.65	6
Kentucky	WTA	628,854	32.68	–	1,202,971	62.52	8
Louisiana	WTA	780,154	38.45	–	1,178,638	58.09	8
Maine (at-large)	CD[b]	352,156	47.84	2	332,418	45.16	–
Maine, 1st	CD[b]	*210,921*	*53.95*	*1*	*154,173*	*39.43*	–

State or district	Electoral method	Hillary Clinton Democratic			Donald Trump Republican		
		#	%	Electoral votes	#	%	Electoral votes
Maine, 2nd	CD[b]	*143,952*	*41.06*	–	*180,665*	*51.53*	1
Maryland	WTA	1,677,928	60.33	10	943,169	33.91	–
Massachusetts	WTA	1,995,196	60.01	11	1,090,893	32.81	–
Michigan	WTA	2,268,839	47.27	–	2,279,543	47.50	16
Minnesota	WTA	1,367,716	46.44	10	1,322,951	44.92	–
Mississippi	WTA	462,127	39.74	–	678,284	58.32	6
Missouri	WTA	1,054,889	37.84	–	1,585,753	56.88	10
Montana	WTA	177,709	35.75	–	279,240	56.17	3
Nebraska (at-lrg)	CD	284,494	33.70	–	495,961	58.75	2

State or district	Electoral method	Hillary Clinton Democratic			Donald Trump Republican		
		#	%	Electoral votes	#	%	Electoral votes
Nebraska, 1st	CD	*100,126*	*35.46*	–	*158,626*	*56.18*	1
Nebraska, 2nd	CD	*131,030*	*44.92*	–	*137,564*	*47.16*	1
Nebraska, 3rd	CD	*53,290*	*19.73*	–	*199,657*	*73.92*	1
Nevada	WTA	539,260	47.92	6	512,058	45.50	–
New Hampshire	WTA	348,526	46.98	4	345,790	46.61	–
New Jersey	WTA	2,148,278	54.99	14	1,601,933	41.00	–
New Mexico	WTA	385,234	48.26	5	319,666	40.04	–
New York	WTA	4,441,437	59.06	29	2,738,645	36.41	–
North Carolina	WTA	2,189,350	46.17	–	2,362,697	49.83	15

State or district	Electoral method	Hillary Clinton Democratic			Donald Trump Republican		
		#	%	Electoral votes	#	%	Electoral votes
North Dakota	WTA	93,758	27.23	–	216,794	62.96	3
Ohio	WTA	2,394,164	43.56	–	2,841,005	51.69	18
Oklahoma	WTA	420,375	28.93	–	949,136	65.32	7
Oregon	WTA	1,002,106	50.07	7	782,403	39.09	–
Pennsylvania	WTA	2,926,457	48.02	–	2,970,764	48.75	20
Rhode Island	WTA	227,062	53.83	4	166,454	39.46	–
South Carolina	WTA	855,373	40.67	–	1,155,389	54.94	9
South Dakota	WTA	117,442	31.74	–	227,701	61.53	3
Tennessee	WTA	868,853	34.90	–	1,519,926	61.06	11

State or district	Electoral method	Hillary Clinton Democratic			Donald Trump Republican		
		#	%	Electoral votes	#	%	Electoral votes
Texas	WTA	3,877,868	43.24	–	4,685,047	52.23	38
Utah	WTA	310,674	27.46	–	515,211	45.54	6
Vermont	WTA	178,573	55.72	3	95,369	29.76	–
Virginia	WTA	1,981,473	49.75	13	1,769,443	44.43	–
Washington	WTA	1,742,718	54.3	12	1,221,747	38.07	–
West Virginia	WTA	188,794	26.48	–	489,371	68.63	5
Wisconsin	WTA	1,382,536	46.45	–	1,405,284	47.22	10
Wyoming	WTA	55,973	21.63	–	174,419	67.40	3
U.S. Total	–	65,758,070	48.07	232	62,916,237	45.99	306

Donald Trump defied the odds all right, won a resounding victory in the 2016 Presidential Election by garnering 306 Electoral votes against Hillary Clinton's 232, much to the consternation of the political elites and financial heavyweights in the USA and the rest of the world, even though he lost by a margin of close to 3 million votes to Hillary Clinton. In fact, he lost the Popular Vote to the Democratic nominee by 62,958,481 to 65,818,412 (i.e. 46.00% to 48.10%). He did so through a brilliant strategy that tapped the realities of the day. His campaign focused more on where the votes mattered in a country where the winner of the highest number of Electoral votes wins the Presidential Election. He did so by not overstretching himself and by employing a deceptive campaign strategy that led his opponents to be wrong in their guess about him all the time.

Why Donald Trump's opponents failed to smell a rat; why they failed to see that there was something unusual in this campaign when forecasts or predictions fell short one after the other, it is difficult to explain. After all, the Republican Party's presidential candidate speedily bounced back from one self-inflicting wound after the other or from setback to setback, even after polls showed him lagging behind his Democratic Party rival with wide margins. Even no-nonsense analysts were seen coming back shortly after the presentations of their damning reports, with new pronouncements stating that Donald Trump caught up again with Hillary Clinton. They even came back declaring that the Republican nominee was leading in some cases. They did so as if dragging their feet or as if feeling uneasy about admitting to the fact that there was a turn-around in events. And they did so in a partisan manner because it was blatant to most of those following the campaign developments that the mainstream media and pollsters did not want Donald Trump to win. However, even right up to the last day, most polls showed Hillary Clinton leading her Republican counterpart. In short, the anomalies seen in the reporting during the Trump-Clinton race led to these unavoidable questions:

- Why was the media found wanting so many times in their predictions?
- Why did pundits fail consistently in analyzing the Trump enigma in a race that everyone agreed had the potential of causing an earthquake in the political setup of America?

We find the answers to the above questions in the ignored, downplayed and underrated aspects of the makeup of America that Donald Trump did a formidable job of tapping, so that not only did they become major and decisive factors in the 2016 Presidential Election, they would forever be recognized in future electoral races as major resources to tap in order to determine the person that would lead the world's last superpower. These factors have been mushrooming or growing rapidly over the past thirty years under different administrations (Republican and Democratic). The mainstream media, the political establishment, the corporations and the financial institutions wanted to keep these factors under wraps, but Donald Trump's victory has brought them to the surface so that they have become fundamental issues that no future presidential aspirant would be able to ignore in the race for the White House.

Table of <u>Presidential Elections</u> by <u>states</u> since 1988
▍Republican win over 5% ▍Republican win under 5%

▌ Democratic win over 5% ▐ Democratic win under 5%
▌ Electoral college winner

Year	1988	1992	1996	2000	2004	2008	2012	2016
Democratic candidate	Michael Dukakis	**Bill Clinton**	**Bill Clinton**	Al Gore	John Kerry	**Barack Obama**	**Barack Obama**	Hillary Clinton
Republican candidate	**George H.W. Bush**	**George H.W. Bush**	Bob Dole	**George W. Bush**	**George W. Bush**	John McCain	Mitt Romney	**Donald Trump**
National popular vote	Bush	Clinton	Clinton	Gore	Bush	Obama	Obama	Clinton
Alabama	Bush	Bush	Dole	Bush	Bush	McCain	Romney	Trump
Alaska	Bush	Bush	Dole	Bush	Bush	McCain	Romney	Trump
Arizona	Bush	Bush	Clinton	Bush	Bush	McCain	Romney	Trump
Arkansas	Bush	Clinton	Clinton	Bush	Bush	McCain	Romney	Trump
California	Bush	Clinton	Clinton	Gore	Kerry	Obama	Obama	Clinton
Colorado	Bush	Clinton	Dole	Bush	Bush	Obama	Obama	Clinton

Connecticut	Bush	Clinton	Clinton	Gore	Kerry	Obama	Obama	Clinton
Delaware	Bush	Clinton	Clinton	Gore	Kerry	Obama	Obama	Clinton
District of Columbia	Dukakis	Clinton	Clinton	Gore	Kerry	Obama	Obama	Clinton
Florida	Bush	Bush	Clinton	Bush	Bush	Obama	Obama	Trump
Georgia	Bush	Clinton	Dole	Bush	Bush	McCain	Romney	Trump
Hawaii	Dukakis	Clinton	Clinton	Gore	Kerry	Obama	Obama	Clinton
Idaho	Bush	Bush	Dole	Bush	Bush	McCain	Romney	Trump
Illinois	Bush	Clinton	Clinton	Gore	Kerry	Obama	Obama	Clinton
Indiana	Bush	Bush	Dole	Bush	Bush	Obama	Romney	Trump
Iowa	Dukakis	Clinton	Clinton	Gore	Bush	Obama	Obama	Trump
Kansas	Bush	Bush	Dole	Bush	Bush	McCain	Romney	Trump
Kentucky	Bush	Clinton	Clinton	Bush	Bush	McCain	Romney	Trump

Louisiana	Bush	Clinton	Clinton	Bush	Bush	McCain	Romney	Trump
Maine	Bush	Clinton	Clinton	Gore Gore (ME-02)	Kerry	Obama	Obama	Clinton Trump (ME-02)
Maryland	Bush	Clinton	Clinton	Gore	Kerry	Obama	Obama	Clinton
Massachusetts	Dukakis	Clinton	Clinton	Gore	Kerry	Obama	Obama	Clinton
Michigan	Bush	Clinton	Clinton	Gore	Kerry	Obama	Obama	Trump
Minnesota	Dukakis	Clinton	Clinton	Gore	Kerry[33]	Obama	Obama	Clinton
Mississippi	Bush	Bush	Dole	Bush	Bush	McCain	Romney	Trump
Missouri	Bush	Clinton	Clinton	Bush	Bush	McCain	Romney	Trump
Montana	Bush	Clinton	Dole	Bush	Bush	McCain	Romney	Trump
Nebraska	Bush	Bush	Dole	Bush	Bush	McCain Obama (NE-02)	Romney	Trump Trump (NE-02)

Nevada	Bush	Clinton	Clinton	Bush	Bush	Obama	Obama	Clinton
New Hampshire	Bush	Clinton	Clinton	Bush	Kerry	Obama	Obama	Clinton
New Jersey	Bush	Clinton	Clinton	Gore	Kerry	Obama	Obama	Clinton
New Mexico	Bush	Clinton	Clinton	Gore	Bush	Obama	Obama	Clinton
New York	Dukakis	Clinton	Clinton	Gore	Kerry	Obama	Obama	Clinton
North Carolina	Bush	Bush	Dole	Bush	Bush	Obama	Romney	Trump
North Dakota	Bush	Bush	Dole	Bush	Bush	McCain	Romney	Trump
Ohio	Bush	Clinton	Clinton	Bush	Bush	Obama	Obama	Trump
Oklahoma	Bush	Bush	Dole	Bush	Bush	McCain	Romney	Trump
Oregon	Dukakis	Clinton	Clinton	Gore	Kerry	Obama	Obama	Clinton
Pennsylvania	Bush	Clinton	Clinton	Gore	Kerry	Obama	Obama	Trump
Rhode Island	Dukakis	Clinton	Clinton	Gore	Kerry	Obama	Obama	Clinton

South Carolina	Bush	Bush	Dole	Bush	Bush	McCain	Romney	Trump
South Dakota	Bush	Bush	Dole	Bush	Bush	McCain	Romney	Trump
Tennessee	Bush	Clinton	Clinton	Bush	Bush	McCain	Romney	Trump
Texas	Bush	Bush	Dole	Bush	Bush	McCain	Romney	Trump
Utah	Bush	Bush	Dole	Bush	Bush	McCain	Romney	Trump
Vermont	Bush	Clinton	Clinton	Gore	Kerry	Obama	Obama	Clinton
Virginia	Bush	Bush	Dole	Bush	Bush	Obama	Obama	Clinton
Washington	Dukakis	Clinton	Clinton	Gore	Kerry	Obama	Obama	Clinton
West Virginia	Dukakis	Clinton	Clinton	Bush	Bush	McCain	Romney	Trump
Wisconsin	Dukakis	Clinton	Clinton	Gore	Kerry	Obama	Obama	Trump
Wyoming	Bush	Bush	Dole	Bush	Bush	McCain	Romney	Trump

This account is not only an examination of the factors or game changers that enabled Donald Trump to win the 2016 Presidential Election, but it is also the careful construction of an idea of how

America can avoid the divisive politics haunting the country in the bid to find a balance between the different interest groups in the American society.

CHAPTER TWO

Ethnicity

Race played a major role in the 2016 Presidential Election. Right up to the closing days of the election campaign, most Americans thought Donald Trump was convinced the United State of America's first black president Barack Obama was not born in the country. In fact, many Americans believed Donald Trump's remarks about blacks, Hispanics, Arabs, and Muslims were racial or had racial undertones in them. So, when he turned around days before election day and declared that Barack Obama was born in the USA, and then went further by asking the population to put the matter to rest once and for all, many people were shocked. They had to be because he had been jabbing the president for years, questioning the legality of him running for the office of president of the United States of America when he "was not American-born".

When people from all of the afore-mentioned racial groups Donald Trump had said things about that the mainstream considered racial, defied the media and then came out and defended him against those who called him a racist, even some of his detractors were forced to think that something about his character more than meets the eye. However, even if we rise above the controversies, one thing we cannot close our eyes to is the fact that the president-elect's politically incorrect statements regarding some of America's minorities created the platform on which he ran his campaign. Yes, Donald J. Trump ran his campaign on the back of White America. Not on mainstream White America that the political establishment had been dealing with over the past decades in a comfortable manner, but on the other half of White America that for years considered itself on the fringes of American politics.

So, the question looms:

- What are the salient aspects of this half of White America that made it possible for Donald Trump to win the 2016 Presidential Election?

To find a better balance between a short but explicit answer to this question and a detailed and insightful reply, I shall begin with the harmonization of different analysis. The media, political pundits, and even the general population analyzed and made predictions on the results of past elections based on the simplified categorization of race as most of us know it today. In fact, the consensus virtually eliminated nuances. Why that is so in a rapidly integrating world where interracial marriages are no longer uncommon, it is difficult to explain.

Demographic	Vote by race				
	White	**Black**	**Hispanic**	**Asian**	**Other**
Trump	58%	8%	29%	29%	37%
Clinton	37%	88%	65%	65%	56%

race and gender

	clinton	trump	other/no answer
white men **34%**	31%	63%	6%
white women **37%**	43%	53%	4%
black men **5%**	80%	13%	7%
black women **7%**	94%	4%	2%
latino men **5%**	62%	33%	5%
latino women **6%**	68%	26%	6%
others **6%**	61%	32%	7%

24537 respondents

The citizens of the United States of America are racially classified today as either White, Hispanic, African, Asian, American, Native-American or American/Pacific/Eskimos. Somebody from South Africa looking at the racial makeup of the USA would think that there are no mixed-race Americans or colored people of the country.

The biggest oversimplification in this grouping of Americans has been the white vote. It stems from the fact that ethnicity is often overlooked or ignored when it comes to White Americans. Statements like "I am Irish", "I am Scottish", "I am German", "I am English", "I am Russian", "I am Polish", "I am Italian" are common among White Americans, often indicating a combination or combinations of the different European origin nationalities. But they are downplayed by statisticians during elections who prefer not to delve deeper and find out the influence voters' ethnic roots have in their choice of candidates during elections. Analysts have always found it convenient to base their predictions on White America by judging this group as a single solid block that makes decisions on how to vote and who to vote for based on standard factors like the economy, immigration, religion, foreign policy and other social concerns. As Steven Seidman, a sociologist and currently a professor at the State University of New York at Albany said:

"Whites are most commonly unaware of their privilege and the way their culture has always been dominant in the US, as they do not identify as members of a specific racial group but rather incorrectly perceive their views and culture as "raceless", when in fact it is ethnonational (ethnic/cultural) specific, with a racial base component."

Language Families in Europe: Green is Germanic (Teutonic), Purple is Romance (Latin), and Red is Slavic.

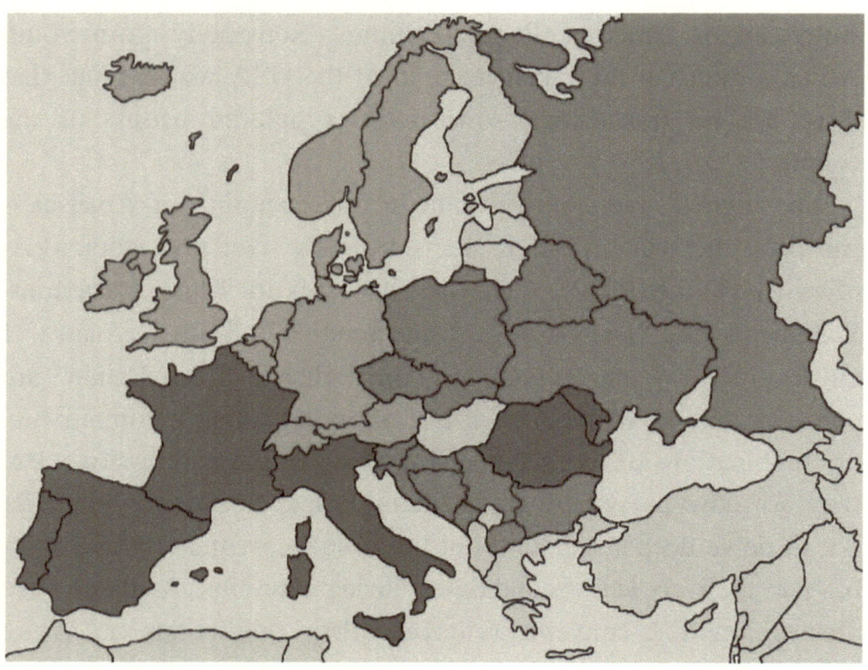

At the turn of the twentieth century, the ethno-linguistic origin of most Caucasoid or White Americans could be traced to a Europe with an ethno-linguistic map that looked like the one above and below.

Ethno-linguistic map of Europe in 1920

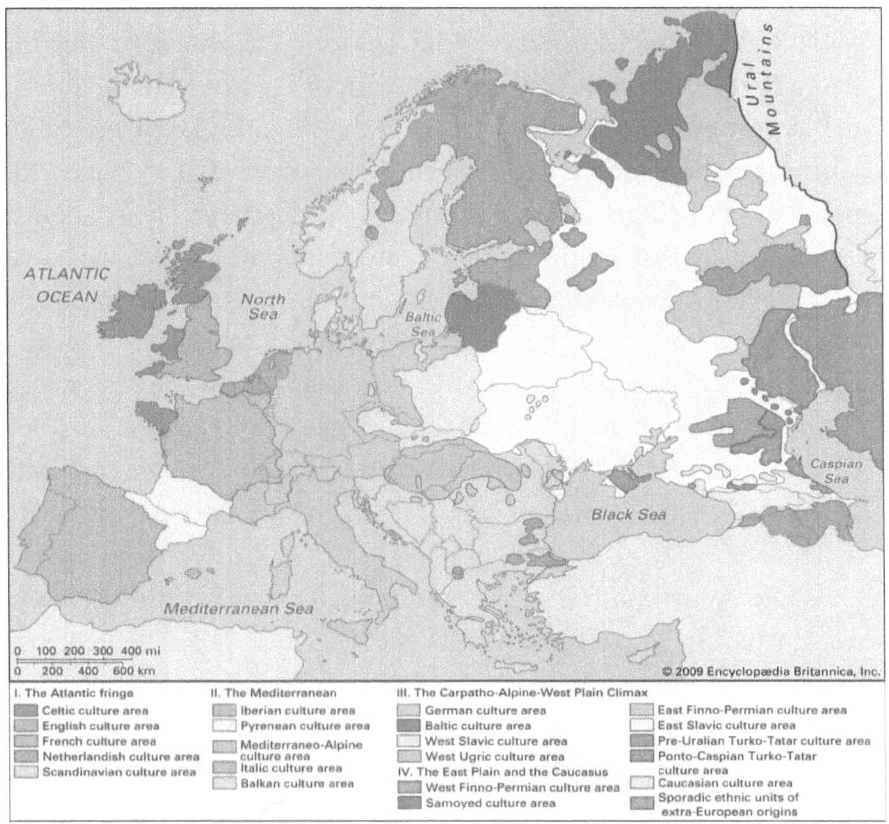

While the racial definition of White in the United States of America elicits muddled responses from a fair percentage of young White Americans, many of whom even think the group is indigenous in the USA, the special status the group reserves for itself has not diminished much over the years.

White Americans (non-Hispanic and Hispanic) accounted for up to 75% of the American population in 2008. Among the White American population, those with German roots constitute the largest ancestry ties or ethnic group or nationality, followed by Irish Americans and English Americans. In the 1980 census, 49,598,035 Americans cited English as their ancestry, making them 26% of the population of the country's white population and the largest ethnic or national group at the time. In fact, the English American population back then was even larger than the population of England itself. But then, twenty years later, slightly more than half of English Americans would cite their ancestry as "American", a phenomenon that has only increased on subsequent censuses. In fact, virtually everywhere that "American" ancestry dominates on the 2000 census corresponds to places where "English" Americans predominated on the 1980 census. This is a clear indication of the fact that there is a more "Native Mindset" among English Americans than among other groups of White Americans.

White Americans (Hispanic and non-Hispanic) are projected to remain the majority, though their percentage is going to decrease to 72% of the total population by 2050. However, projections state that non-Hispanic White Americans of that group will become less than 50% of the population of the USA by 2042 mainly because Non-Hispanic White Americans have the lowest fertility rate of any major racial group in the country. This low birth rate among White Americans is compounded by the mass-immigration of other ethnic groups with higher birth rates, and the high rate of intermarriage this non-Hispanic White group with Hispanic White Americans.

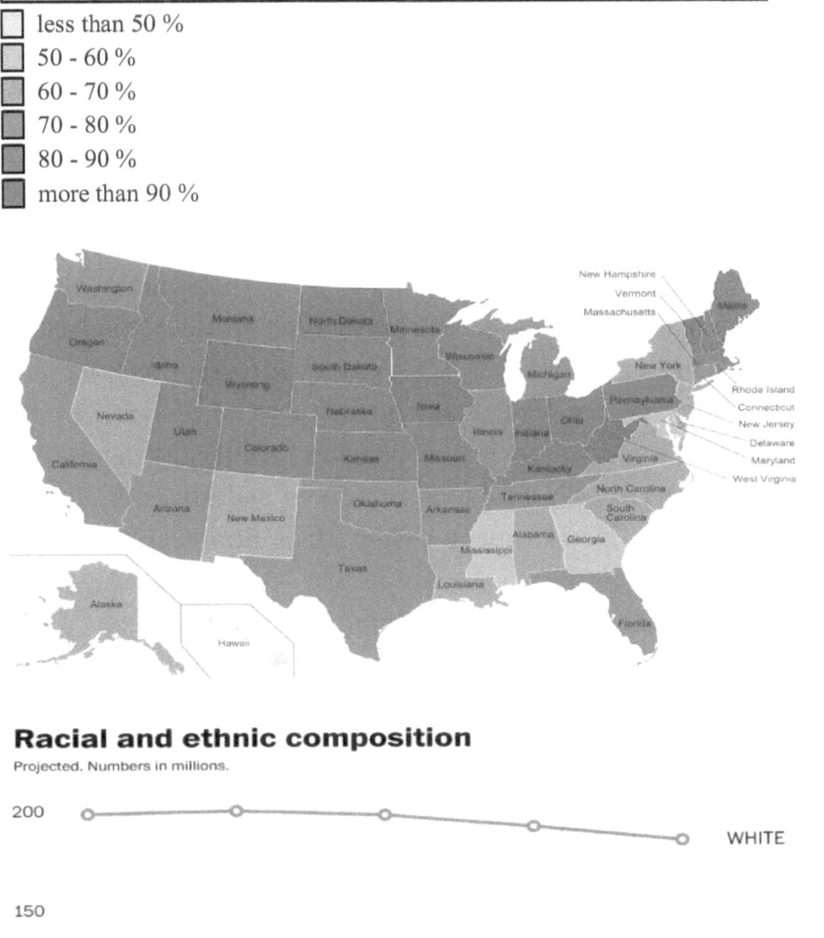

Racial and ethnic composition

Projected. Numbers in millions.

Population-wise, Americans of English origin are the largest ethnonational group among White Americans since they numbered 49,598,035 in 1980, compared with 49,224,146 Americans of German origin, 40,165,702 of Irish origin, and 12,183,692 of Italian origin.

However, the decrease in the number of White Americans of English origin from 49,598,035 in 1980 to 24,382,182 in 2014 is due to the fact that more and more English Americans are choosing to identify themselves simply as Americans. Expanding on the explanation made before, it is obvious that the "Native Mindset" is becoming more fashionable in a rapidly integrating America, and English Americans are leading this growing trend of US. Citizens who were born and raised in the country identifying themselves simply as "Americans", unlike their parents and ancestors before them. This contrasts with many of the other European American ethnicities.

Today we have the leading ethnic groups among White Americans being German Americans (14.4%), Irish Americans (10.4%), English Americans (7.6%) and Italian Americans (5.4%).

- Where did this "Native Mindset" come from?
- How did it shape the political thinking in America?
- And how did it influence the 2016 Presidential Election?

Well over ten million White Americans can trace part of their ancestry back to the Pilgrims (religious congregations of Brownest English Dissenters who had fled the volatile political environment in England for the relative calm and tolerance of 16th–17th century Holland, in the Netherlands) who arrived on the Mayflower in 1620. These Calvinists along with the descendants of the Puritans (a group of English Reformed Protestants who sought to "purify" the Church of England from its "Catholic" practices in the 16th and

17th centuries) who left England for America, form the core of English Americans and what plainly is known today as "Americans". The two groups from England are the core of what became known as WASP (White Anglo-Saxon Protestant), which forms the majority and the cream of the political class in the USA since its founding on July 4, 1776. In fact, Americans of English origin abound in both the Republican and the Democratic Parties and constitute the nucleus of what is considered the elites of the political establishment. Besides Martin Van Buren of Dutch origin, and John Fitzgerald Kennedy, a legend of Irish descent who served as the 35th President of the United States of America from January 20, 1961–November 22, 1963, all past US. presidents have either been full-blooded or mix-blooded English Americans.

There are muted talks of a sense of entitlement among Anglo-Saxon Americans and of a feeling among some of them that other White American groups are a threat to their status. Anglo-Saxon bashers even claim that this sense of entitlement among Americans of English origin is centuries old. In fact, in the eighteenth century, Benjamin Franklin, one of America's iconic founding fathers, warned some of the other founding fathers about the threat to the status quo posed by German immigrants whom he thought were overrunning America. In this insightful piece attributed to Benjamin Franklin, he wrote:

Why should Pennsylvania, founded by the English, become a Colony of Aliens, who will shortly be so numerous as to Germanize us instead of our Anglifying them, and will never adopt our Language or Customs, any more than they can acquire our Complexion?

24. Which leads me to add one Remark: That the Number of purely white People in the World is proportionately very small. All Africa is black or tawny. Asia chiefly tawny. America (exclusive of the newcomers) wholly so. And in Europe, the Spaniards, Italians,

French, Russians, and Swedes, are generally of what we call a swarthy Complexion; as are the Germans also, the Saxons only excepted, who with the English, make the principal Body of White People on the Face of the Earth. I could wish their Numbers were increased. And while we are, as I may call it, scouring our Planet, by clearing America of Woods, and so making this Side of our Globe reflect a brighter Light to the Eyes of Inhabitants in Mars or Venus, why should we in the Sight of Superior Beings, darken its People? why increase the Sons of Africa, by Planting them in America, where we have so fair an Opportunity, by excluding all Blacks and Tawneys, of increasing the lovely White and Red? But perhaps I am partial to the Complexion of my Country, for such Kind of Partiality is natural to Mankind.

While the racial definition of White in the United States of America elicits muddled responses from a fair percentage of young White Americans, many of whom even think the group is indigenous in the USA, the special status the group reserves for itself has not diminished much over the years.

Benjamin Franklin would have been appalled by Donald Trump's win were he alive today. When confronted with the reality that the Republican president-elect is of German roots from his father's side and of Scottish roots from his mother's side, ethnic groups or nationalities that Anglo-Saxons looked down on in the past, Benjamin Franklin would not have been spared of the negative feelings harbored by those who still think Anglo-Saxons are a special or exceptional people. After all, back then, being a pure Anglo-Saxon automatically established someone as an accepted member of America's ruling class. It has been so ever since, but the potency of that inheritance has greatly diminished to the point where "Anglo-Saxon Sacredness" is now an imaginary construct. This is particularly so since the number of Anglo-Saxons keep shrinking from intermarriage, loss of Anglo-Saxon consciousness (Americanism) and the indefensibility of the idea of Anglo-Saxon exclusiveness.

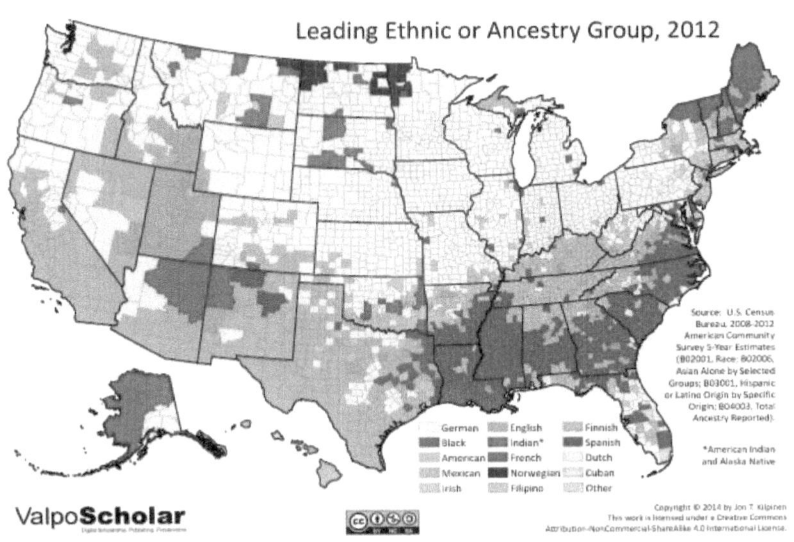

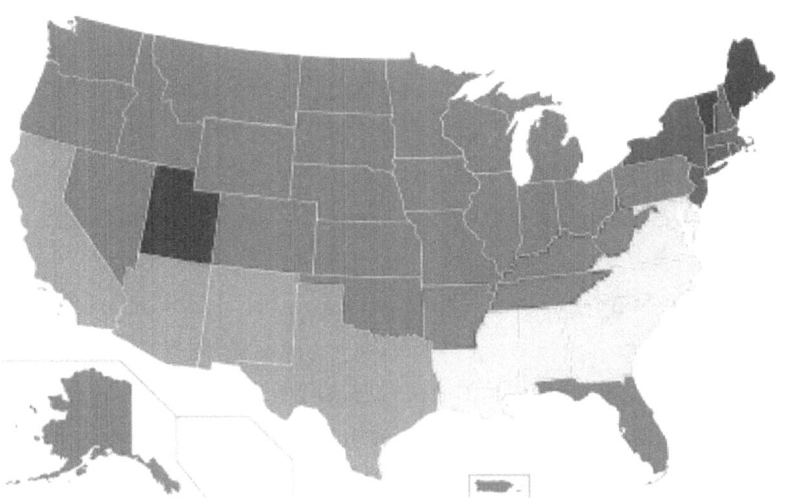

Plurality ancestry in each <u>state</u>, ranging from 11.8% (FL) to 43.9 % (ND).

Donald Trump counted enormously on the backing of America's largest or second largest white group (German Americans) that never commanded political power, got scarred by the horrors of Nazism and German atrocities during the Second World War, and chose to play a subdued role in America's political life. He also counted on Scottish Americans (the fifth largest White American group that was 10 million strong in 1980, but that is now registered as a group made up of 5,365,154 living souls). These two groups voted overwhelmingly for him.

Slavic Americans supported Donald Trump too. After all, his first wife, as well as his third wife, are Slavic (Ivanna hails from the Western Slavic country of Czechoslovakia and Melania is from the small Southern Slavic country of Slovenia). It is not a secret at all that Slavs (the largest Indo-European ethno-linguistic group in Europe) have a peculiar solidarity uncommon among many other European ethno-linguistic groups. Numbering some 18–18.5 million (6% of the population of the USA and close to 10% of the white population), Americans of Slavic origin, of which ethnic Russians are the majority, are increasingly becoming a powerful factor to reckon with in American politics. And since most Americans with Slavic roots do not view Russia and its President Vladimir Putin as an enemy or a threat to the United States of America, with the exception of Polish Americans, it is understandable why Donald Trump's peaceful overture to Russia was well-received by Slavic American voters, who unlike most other ethno-linguistic groups in the USA, thought the anti-Russian and anti-Putin messages streaming out of the mainstream media and flooding the internet stemmed more from hysteria than from anything else.

Some Slav rubbed off Donald Trump, some of his Slavic supporters say. Why not? Others would ask. Well, perhaps the president-elect understands Slavs and Slavic Americans better than most of the Anglo-Saxon elites and the other Anglophiles of the political establishment. After all, through marriage and the children that came out of those marriages, he has every reason to cherish his ties to Slavs and the Slavic world of which Russia is the big brother.

It is tempting to think that most Americans do not understand Europe's ethno-linguistic composition, and that very few of them pay attention to the subtle influences it has among White Americans today. It is even more tempting to think that an even smaller number of the consultants in both the Trump and Clinton campaign teams imagined Donald Trump's Scottish side would increase his political leverage the way it did. But it did play an outsized role not only among Americans of full or partial Scottish origin, but also among Irish, Welsh and even Breton Americans, who like the Scots are Celtic, and who like them also, treasure their common Celtic origin. Americans of Celtic roots who in many ways are outsiders when it comes to the core of the American political establishment played a formidable role in the Midwest in tilting the Electoral vote towards Donald Trump's favor, and their collective position on any issue will henceforth be taken seriously by the political establishment.

It is obvious that the Celtic factor is the principal reason why so many predictions made by renowned individuals and institutions of the past went awry, leaving the media and political pundits scratching their heads in puzzlement after election day. The majority of Celtic Americans who also happen to be overwhelmingly Catholic, undoubtedly found "one of their own" in Donald Trump, and so gave his campaign a special flavor, and then voted for him accordingly.

And by consciously tapping Catholic solidarity that is strong among Italians, Scottish Americans, Welsh Americans and Irish

Americans, Donald Trump combined religion and ethnicity in an effective manner to garner far more the support from White America's minorities than previous Republican presidential candidates ever got from these minorities, thereby making this election in its simplified form as a battle between the Anglo-Saxon White Americans and their associates who have been dominating the political establishment versus the majority non-Anglo-Saxon White Americans who could be considered a disgruntled lot that think they have been left out for too long in the cold of America's political life.

The above explanations among other things make it unsurprising that Donald Trump successfully neutralized the Hillary Clinton campaign in the previously Democratic-leaning States of Wisconsin, Michigan, Illinois, Ohio, Pennsylvania—states where German Americans are the majority of the population of White Americans. It is here that an unconscious alliance emerged between German Americans that are the most populous in this area and Americans of Slavic and Celtic roots.

The political establishment dominated by politicians of Anglo-Saxon roots, an establishment whose core is the Democratic Party and the Republican Party elites that secretly or openly supported Hillary Clinton, ended up getting most of their white votes from Anglo-Saxon Americans, White Latino-Americans, Asian Americans, African Americans, Native Americans and other minorities. In a nutshell, ancestry or the ethno-linguistic roots of voters played a significant role or counted a lot in the choice of candidate to vote for in the 2016 Presidential Election. That many of those who were conscious of their roots contributed enormously to Donald Trump's electoral victory, especially in America's Midwestern States dominated by the Rustbelt, says a lot and gives pundits more reason to delve deeper into this factor in future Presidential Elections.

Ancestral Roots of White Americans

Ancestral origin	1980	%	1990	%	2000	%
Albanian	38,658	0.02%	47,710	0.02%	113,661	0.04%
American	-	-	12,395,999	5.0%	20,188,305	7.2%
Armenian	214,362	0.09%	296,672	0.1%	385,488	0.1%
Austrian	948,558	0.42%	864,783	0.3%	730,336	0.3%
Azerbaijani	4,563	0.002%	12,737	0.01%	24,377	0.01%
Basque	43,140	0.02%	47,956	0.02%	57,793	0.02%
Belarusian	-	-	-	-	25,639	0.2%
Belgian	360,277	0.16%	380,403	0.2%	348,531	0.1%

Bosnian	-	-	-	-	350,000	0.1%
British	-	-	1,119,140	0.4%	1,085,718	0.4%
Bulgarian	42,504	0.02%	29,595	0.01%	55,489	0.02%
Catalan	-	-	-	-	1,738	-
Croatian	252,970	0.11%	544,270	0.2%	374,241	0.1%
Cypriot			4,897		7,643	
Czech	1,892,456	0.84%	1,296,369	0.5%	1,258,452	0.4%
Danish	1,518,273	0.67%	1,634,648	0.7%	1,430,897	0.5%
Dutch	6,304,499	2.78%	6,226,339	2.5%	4,541,770	1.6%
English	49,598,035	21.89%	32,651,788	13.1%	24,509,692	8.7%
Estonian	25,994	0.01%	26,762	0.01%	25,034	0.01%
Finnish	615,872	0.27%	658,854	0.3%	623,559	0.2%

French: (incl:*Cors..*) (except Basque)	12,892,246	5.69%	10,320,656	4.1%	13,172,178	4.0%
Georgian					6,298	
German: (incl:*Amish, Tex.*)	49,224,146	21.73%	57,947,171	23.3%	42,841,569	15.2%
Greek	959,856	0.42%	1,110,292	0.4%	1,153,295	0.4%
Hungarian	1,776,902	0.78%	1,582,302	0.6%	1,398,702	0.5%
Icelandic	32,586	0.01%	40,529	0.02%	42,716	0.01%
Irish	40,165,702	17.73%	38,735,539	15.6%	30,524,799	10.8%
Italian: (incl: *Sicilian*)	12,183,692	5.38%	14,664,189	5.9%	15,638,348	5.6%
Latvian	92,141	0.04%	100,331	0.04%	87,564	0.03%

Liechtenstein er	-	-	-	-	1,244	0.0004
Lithuanian	742,776	0.33%	811,865	0.3%	659,992	0.2%
Luxembourg	-	-	-	-	45,139	0.01%
Macedonia	-	-	-	-	57,200	0.02%
Maltese	31,645	0.01%	39,600	0.02%	40,159	0.01%
Moldovan	-	-	-	-	7,859	0.003
Monégasque	-	-	-	-	486	
Montenegrin	-	-	-	-	2,528	0.03%
Norwegian	3,453,839	1.52%	3,869,395	1.6%	4,477,725	1.6%
Pennsylvania Dutch	-	-	-	-	255,807	0.1%
Polish	8,228,037	3.63%	9,366,051	3.8%	8,977,235	3.2%
Portuguese	1,024,351	0.45%	1,148,857	0.5%	1,173,691	0.4%

Romanian	315,258	0.14%	365,531	0.1%	367,278	0.1%
Russian	2,781,432	1.23%	2,951,373	1.2%	2,652,214	0.9%
Scots-Irish	16,418	0.007%	5,617,773	2.3%	4,319,232	1.5%
Scottish	10,048,816	4.44%	5,393,581	2.2%	4,890,581	1.7%
Serbian	100,941	0.04%	116,795	0.05%	51,679	0.05%
Slovak	776,806	0.3%	1,882,897	0.8%	797,764	0.3%
Slovene	126,463	0.06	124,437	0.1%	176,691	0.1%
Sammarinese	-	-	-	-	538	
Spanish:*(incl: Ast., Can., Hisp.)*	94,52	0.1%	360,935		299,948	
Swedish	4,345,392	1.92%	4,680,863	1.9%	3,998,310	1.4%
Swiss	981,543	0.43%	1,045,492	0.4%	911,502	0.3%
Turkish	75,988	0.03%	86,427	0.17%	117,575	0.1%

JANVIER T. CHANDO

Ukrainian	730,056	0.32%	740,723	0.3%	892,922	0.3%
Welsh	1,664,598	0.73%	2,033,893	0.82%	1,753,794	0.6%
Yugoslavian	-	-	-	-	328,547	0.1%
Other European	-	-	-	-	1,968,696	0.7%
Scandinavian	-	-	-	-	425,099	0.2%
United States total	214,726,269	94.78%	223,371,445	89.81%	201,290,597	71.53 %

CHAPTER THREE

Immigration

Drawing from the words attributed to Benjamin Franklin concerning the non-conformist or alien nature of the German immigrants in his day, and drawing as well from the words and actions of other politicians who came after him down the centuries and decades, words highlighting their discomfort with the "Others", meaning the new immigrant groups that had not yet assimilated into the "American Way of Life", we can conclude that America is a country with a very strong "Nativist Tradition".

The United States of America is a country of immigrants all right, but it is a country that got molded during its entire history to reflect the notion that those American citizens who were born in the USA, raised here or who have their ancestral roots here in America (Amerindians, Eskimos etc.) are "not immigrants", even if part(s) of their ethnic roots are out of the country.

U.S. IMMIGRATION FROM 1820

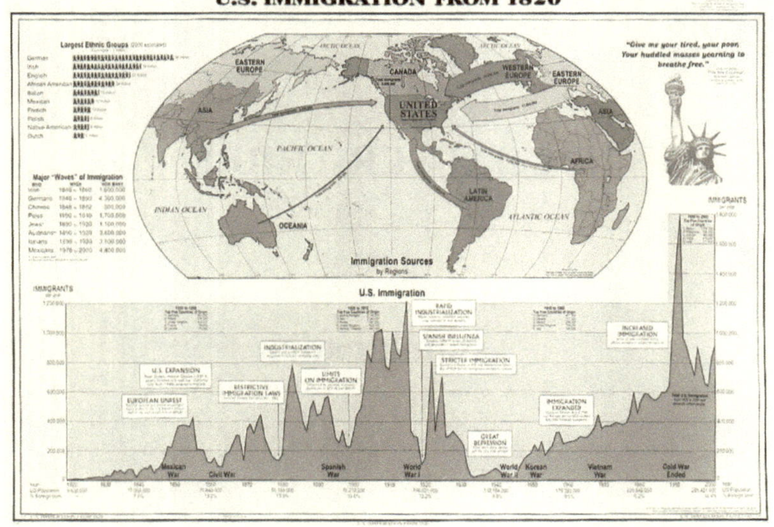

NET INTERNATIONAL MIGRATION

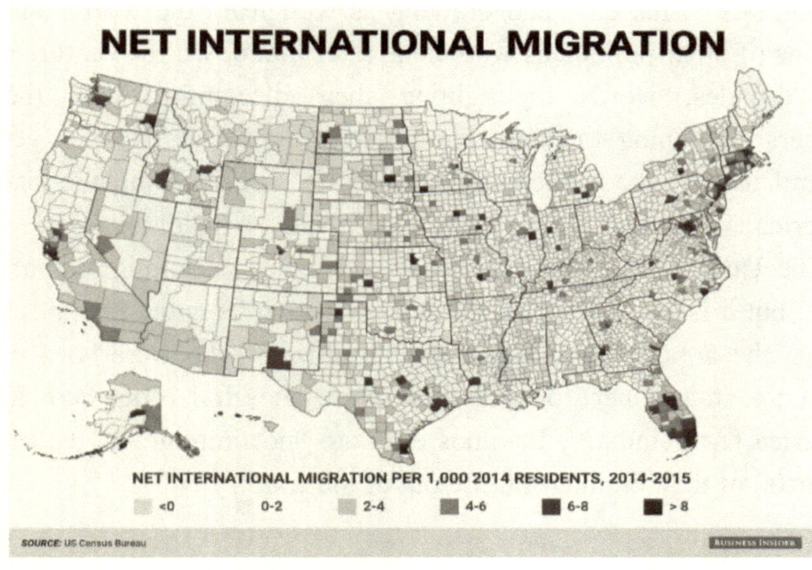

This Nativist Tradition may be viewed as discriminatory, but it comes with a positive side in the sense that the descendants of American citizens of immigrant background automatically become American nativists themselves. This can be seen in the case of Irish Americans today, a people whose history in America is highlighted by the ripple effect of "The Great Famine" or the "Great Hunger" that arose from the potato blight that hit Ireland in 1845-1852, causing mass starvation and disease, and sparking off an unprecedented emigration that saw the United States of America receiving most of these impoverished and starving Irish men, women, and children into the new country, a flood that was initially met with resentment from the other established American populations of European roots. Polish Americans, Italian Americans and Jewish Americans also faced some degree of pushback from the other European ethno-linguistic groups who were already calling America their fatherland and harbored the "Nativist Mindset". However, the quick assimilation of the new immigrant populations into the American way of life made them nativists in no time, so that today, they constitute firm features of the American socio-cultural, economic and political landscape.

Rate of immigration to the United States relative to the population size of the sending country, 2006–2010

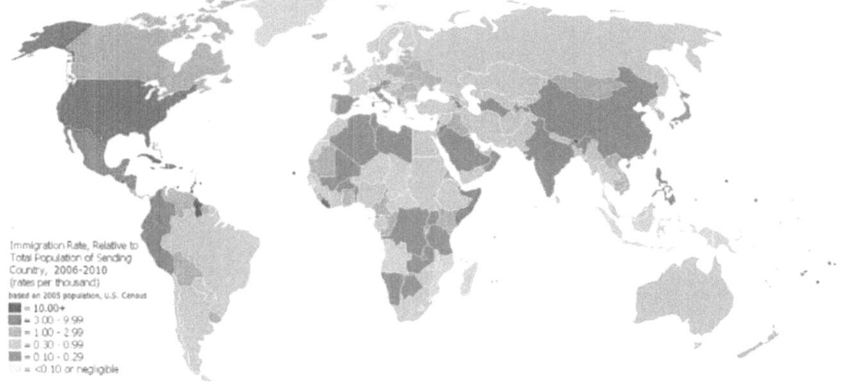

The share of the Foreign-Born Population

Year	Number of foreign-born	Percent foreign-born
1850	2,244,602	9.7
1860	4,138,697	13.2
1870	5,567,229	14.4
1880	6,679,943	13.3
1890	9,249,547	14.8
1900	10,341,276	13.6
1910	13,515,886	14.7
1920	13,920,692	13.2
1930	14,204,149	11.6

Year	Number of foreign-born	Percent foreign-born
1940	11,594,896	8.8
1950	10,347,395	6.9
1960	9,738,091	5.4
1970	9,619,302	4.7
1980	14,079,906	6.2
1990	19,767,316	7.9
2000	31,107,889	11.1
2010	39,956,000	12.9

Country of birth of foreign-born population of the United States of America in 2013 (<u>U.S. Census Bureau</u>) and number of immigrants between 1986 and 2012 by country of birth

Countries included in the table exceed 50,000 in either category.

Country of birth	Population (2013)	Immigrants (1986-2012)
<u>**United States**</u>	*316,497,531*	*3,132*
Total foreign born	*41,347,945*	*26,147,963*
<u>Mexico</u>	11,584,977	5,551,757
<u>China</u>	2,383,831	1,399,667
<u>India</u>	2,034,677	1,323,011
<u>Philippines</u>	1,843,989	1,480,946
<u>Vietnam</u>	1,281,010	955,967
<u>El Salvador</u>	1,252,067	676,776
<u>Cuba</u>	1,144,024	666,657

Country of birth	Population (2013)	Immigrants (1986-2012)
South Korea	1,070,335	609,321
Dominican Republic	991,046	904,721
Guatemala	902,293	353,122
Canada	840,192	394,790
Jamaica	714,743	507,741
United Kingdom	695,489	383,037
Colombia	677,231	498,551
Haiti	593,980	536,657
Germany	584,184	192,676
Honduras	533,598	178,321

Country of birth	Population (2013)	Immigrants (1986-2012)
Peru	440,292	320,611
Poland	432,601	360,669
Ecuador	427,906	243,217
Russia	390,934	476,306
Iran	363,972	358,586
Italy	354,305	69,111
Ukraine	345,187	306,203
Pakistan	342,603	347,237
Japan	339,970	172,893
Brazil	337,040	214,266

Country of birth	Population (2013)	Immigrants (1986-2012)
Guyana	259,815	214,995
Nicaragua	240,619	191,701
Nigeria	234,465	227,497
Thailand	233,547	174,168
Trinidad and Tobago	232,026	157,689
Bangladesh	203,179	215,164
Iraq	200,894	153,897
Venezuela	197,724	143,411
Laos	196,154	110,235
Ethiopia	195,805	202,518

Country of birth	Population (2013)	Immigrants (1986-2012)
Portugal	182,473	53,831
Egypt	176,443	153,755
France	170,394	87,601
Argentina	170,086	98,999
Cambodia	164,746	106,183
Romania	157,302	140,887
Ghana	149,377	130,542
Greece	137,084	37,406
Republic of Ireland	128,350	104,586
Israel	127,079	106,568

Country of birth	Population (2013)	Immigrants (1986-2012)
Lebanon	124,256	113,727
Burma	116,775	94,792
Bosnia and Herzegovina	112,240	129,481
Kenya	110,678	92,891
Turkey	109,667	85,415
Spain	102,475	41,328
Panama	101,024	57,628
Chile	97,585	54,573
South Africa	95,191	69,992
Indonesia	94,600	61,493

Country of birth	Population (2013)	Immigrants (1986-2012)
Saudi Arabia	88,894	n/a
Nepal	87,456	58,841
Netherlands	85,085	35,117
Albania	81,047	84,031
Bolivia	79,924	52,177
Armenia	79,122	62,201
Syria	78,934	68,864
Liberia	78,909	74,632
Australia	78,797	12,926
Costa Rica	78,659	47,648

Country of birth	Population (2013)	Immigrants (1986-2012)
Hungary	74,213	31,365
Malaysia	68,956	n/a
Bulgaria	67,941	68,768
Afghanistan	67,169	59,480
Jordan	65,618	104,168
Czech Republic	64,354	27,354
Morocco	63,798	76,622
Barbados	52,499	25,444
Sri Lanka	51,268	51,675
Belarus	50,934	58,254

Country of birth	Population (2013)	Immigrants (1986-2012)
Belize	50,296	n/a

Note: Counts of immigrants since 1986 for Russia includes "Soviet Union (former)", and for Czech Republic includes "Czechoslovakia (former)"

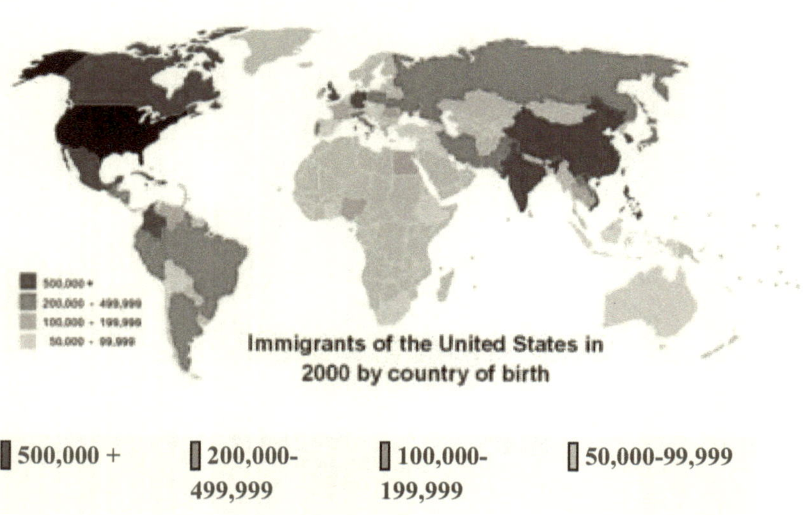

| 500,000 + | 200,000-499,999 | 100,000-199,999 | 50,000-99,999 |

So, it is not surprising that the picture presented by some of the extremists or right-wing groups that supported Donald Trump was of an America and Americans being overwhelmed by increasing immigrant populations of Muslims, Chinese, Hispanics (Mexicans), etc. so that the country is being taken away from "Real Americans" or the nativists. What most liberals, moderates, and even some conservatives find surprising about the manifestations of these anti-immigrant groups is their audacity in unabashedly peddling their preconceived notions that have no place in the twenty-first-century world that is rapidly globalizing.

Another curious thing about the whole melodrama is the fact that the overwhelming majority of those who consider themselves "Real Americans" are mostly White Americans, a fair percentage of whom have extreme views on race, immigration, and religion. Though Donald Trump never echoed their extreme sentiments, the white nationalist groups that supported him during the election campaigns did not hide their worries that unchecked immigration would make the non-Hispanic white population a minority in the United States of America a few decades down the road. This is an impending reality anyway as non-Hispanic White Americans intermarry with other races, and as birthrates and fertility rates of non-Hispanic White Americans drop, especially in the northeastern and southeastern states of the country. The anti-Trump mainstream media used the fact that immigration is speeding up the proportionate decline of White Americans in the demography of the country to court the immigrant vote and to further explain the generalized anger at almost everything that has been coming from mostly White males. Irrespective of how the anger of these White males is described, one thing for sure is that the Anglo-Saxon-dominated political establishment is the focal point of their anger.

Donald Trump may have tapped the worry of the demographic decline of White Americans, not by being forthright in pointing out the disadvantages, threats or setbacks that this racial group will encounter in the future because of the decline of their share of the US. population, but by attributing certain negative behaviors to the so-called threatening groups among America's minorities—Mexicans being involved in crime and rape, Chinese undermining America's economy etc. are some of the examples of the passions he stirred with his negative attributes. Nasty as some of the comments about these groups were, those vulnerable to hate and fear took his words to heart and supported him even more. Why he won, especially on the immigration factor, was because his gains from his immigration rhetoric offset the loss of the immigrant vote.

Yes, Donald Trump's strong stance on immigration was a natural turn off for most immigrant communities, especially Hispanics who are America's fastest-growing demographic group. While his message resonated with a few Hispanics, it sounded threatening to the majority, especially the illegal immigrants or families whose loved ones are not legal or are unlikely to regularize their stay in the USA. Numbering about 57 million, America's fastest-growing demographic group took less than 20 years to double its population from 22 million in 1990 to 50 million in 2010, a feat seen only in the fastest growing population centers (countries) of the world, which are mostly in Asia and Sub-Saharan Africa. However, most of the Hispanic vote, especially the Mexican vote, dominates in the states bordering Mexico. It is also good to remember that Hispanics have traditionally supported the Democratic party. After all, most Hispanics happen to be Catholics and Catholics traditionally voted the Democratic Party until this election. Why Catholics related to Donald Trump based on religion in this election, can be further explained by other related factors.

One place that stood out for its peculiarity was Florida. Here, Hispanics make up 22.5% of the state's population of 20 million. The largest groups among the Hispanic population are 6.5% (1,213,438) Cuban, 4.5% (847,550) Puerto Rican, 3.3% (629,718) Mexican, and 1.6% (300,414) Colombian. Donald Trump's promise to abrogate the peace agreement the Obama administration worked out with the Castro government of Cuba, a government loathed by most of Florida's Cuban Americans and their descendants who consider themselves exiles of Marxist Cuba, is something appealing to Cuban Americans. It was this electoral pledge that contributed enormously to Donald Trump's high performance among voters from the Cuban community, who gave him far more votes than what previous Republican candidates received in past elections.

            JANVIER T. CHANDO

The Size and Share of the Immigrant Population in the USA (U.S. Census Bureau's 2010 and 2014 American Community Surveys (ACS))

Year	Size of Immigrant Population (Millions)	Immigrant Share of Total U.S. Population (%)
1970	9.6	4.7
1980	14.1	6.2
1990	19.8	7.9
2000	31.1	11.1
2010	40.0	12.9
2014	42.4	13.3

CHAPTER FOUR

Electoral College/Popular Vote Disconnect

The rest of the world often marvels at the US. electoral system, especially when it comes to its presidential electoral system where the Electoral vote count more than the Popular Vote. In fact, the majority in virtually every country of the world considers it an anachronism that has managed to survive the passing years, a relic of a misconceived 18th-century, slavery-era, state-by-state, a winner-take-all system for selecting the president of the United States of America that should have no place in the modern world. These foreign entities—both pro-democracy and anti-democracy forces, agree that the Electoral College process which the Founding Fathers established in the Constitution as a compromise between the election of the President by a vote in Congress and the election of the President by a Popular Vote of qualified citizens— gives democracy a bad name in the modern era and that it should be scrapped altogether. Most Americans agree too, and Hillary Clinton is or was one of those who wanted to see those changes.

In fact, in November 2000, just after winning the race to

become the Senator of New York, the bright-faced Hilary Clinton announced that she would introduce a constitutional amendment that would see to the abolition of the Electoral College, a promise she never pursued, and something she regrets not doing because the very Electoral College process just deprived her of becoming the first female president of the United States of America had her victory in the Popular Vote in the 2016 Presidential Election been the only determinant in the race.

US. Map and its constituent states

Changes to the Electoral map

The electoral map in <u>2008</u>.

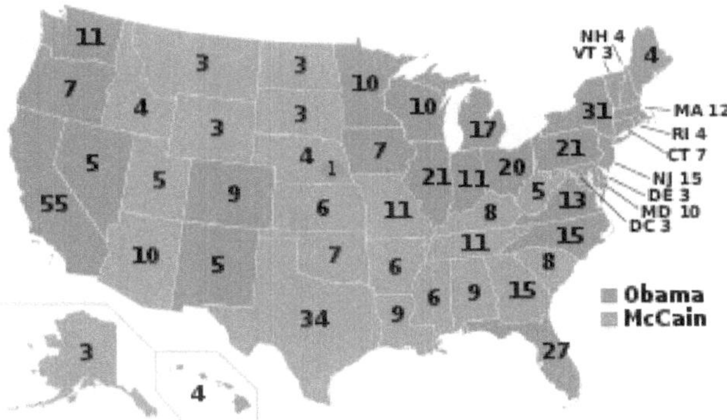

Changes in Electoral vote after the <u>2010 census</u>.

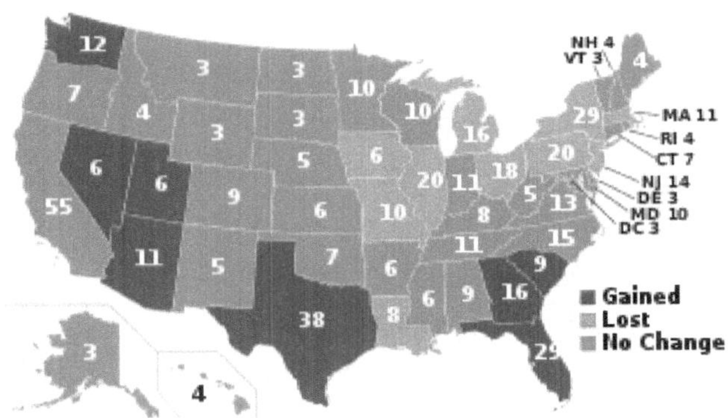

The Electoral Map—Electoral votes per

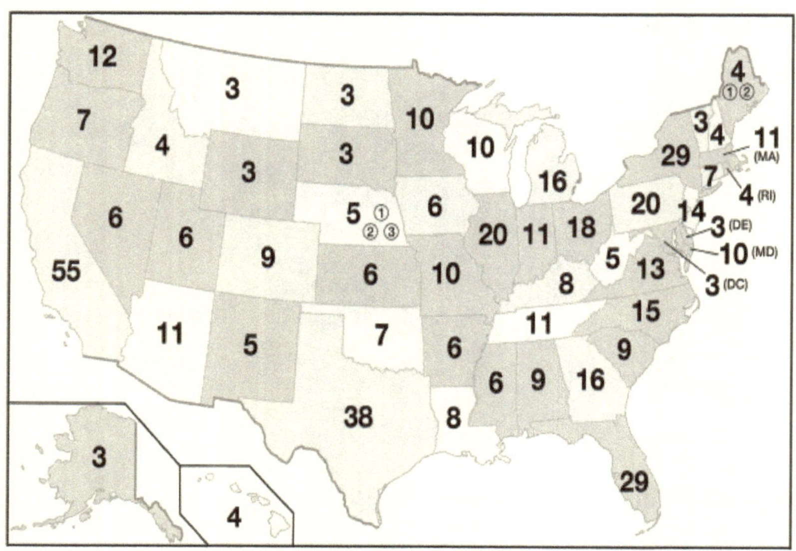

A small peek at the results of the last election shows that Hillary Clinton won 65,736,140 of the Popular Vote against Donald Trump's 62,895,938, giving her 48% of the votes against Donald Trump's 46%. The fact that she had this margin of close to 3 million votes over her Republican rival, yet lost the election due to the Electoral College process, which gave Donald Trump 306 Electoral votes and apportioned 232 to her on November 09, 2016, left a feeling of political rancor among her supporters. 538 electors make up the Electoral College. To elect the President, a majority of 270 or more Electoral votes is required. This explains why Electoral College-wise, Donald Trump had a landslide victory over Hillary Clinton.

Broadly speaking, many of those who believe in popular democracy consider Donald Trump's victory, which came on the back of the Electoral College, a sacrilege that deserves not only to be overturned, but that should never be allowed to repeat itself again. Yet Hillary Clinton is not the only candidate in the history of the United States of America that won the Popular Vote and lost the Electoral College. It happened before in 1824 to John Quincy Adams, in 1876 to Samuel J. Tilden, in 1888 to Grover Cleveland, and in 2000 to Albert Gore, Jr. However, what is peculiar about this travesty of popular democracy is the fact that the victims of the Electoral College twist have always been Democratic Party nominees. So, it is understandable why more than 70% of Democrats and Hillary Clinton supporters consider the Electoral College process an unfair process and wish to see it reformed or abolished altogether. This is an upswing from 66% based on a 2013 Gallup poll. In fact, back then, most Americans irrespective of the political parties they were affiliated to, supported doing away with the Electoral College.

Americans' Support for Doing Away With U.S. Electoral College

Would you vote for or against a law that would do away with the Electoral College and base the election of the president on the total vote cast throughout the nation?

	Would vote "for" doing away with Electoral College	Would vote "against" doing away with Electoral College	No opinion
	%	%	%
National adults	63	29	8
Republicans	61	30	9
Independents	63	29	8
Democrats	66	30	4
18 to 29 years	69	28	4
30 to 49 years	62	27	11
50 to 64 years	64	28	8
65 and older	60	32	8

Jan. 8-9, 2013

GALLUP

A deeper appraisal of the mechanism for apportioning the Electoral votes reveals that it is not accurate, especially since demography, and more precisely, the population of a state is highly considered in deciding the number of Electoral votes the state gets. Yet, there are many mismatches between states when comparing their populations and their number of Electoral votes. The most glaring disparity is between California and Wyoming. As of July 2014, California has a population of 38,802,500 (12.18% of the total population of the USA), and has 55 Electoral votes (a share of 10.22 of the Total Electoral vote), giving it a ratio of 1 Electoral vote per 691,662 inhabitants. Wyoming, which is the smallest of all the US. States population-wise counts 584,153 souls within its borders (0.18% of the total US. Population), and boasts of 3 Electoral votes (0.56% of the Total Electoral votes), giving it a ratio of 192,137 people per Electoral vote. This discrepancy is not seen only between California and Wyoming. It abounds as the table below shows.

So, it is easy to deduce from the above information why Hillary Clinton won the popular vote and lost the Electoral Vote. She won hugely in states where the ratio of Electoral votes to the size of the population is much higher.

Population Map of the States in 2013

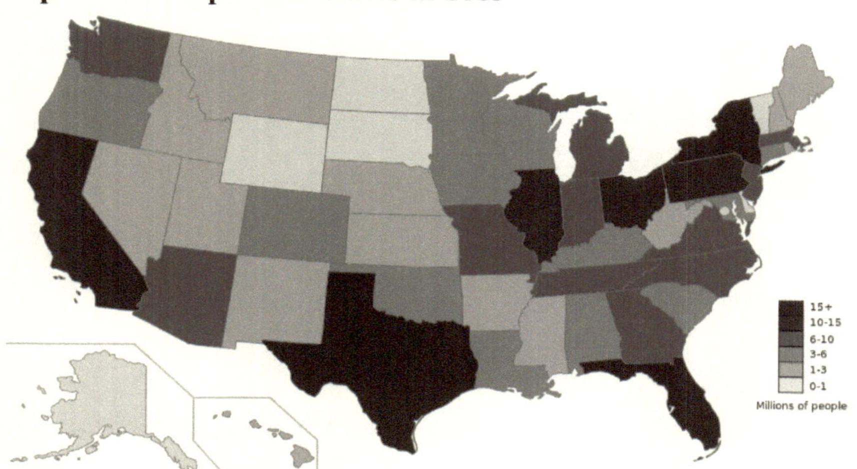

State Population and Electoral votes—July 1, 2014, estimate.

RANK	State	Population	House Seats	Elect. Votes	Pop. per House Seat	Pop. per Elect. Vote	Pop. per Senate Seat	% of Total US Pop	% of Total Elect. Vote
1	California	38,802,500	53	55	717,763	691,662	19,401,250	12.18	10.22
2	Texas	26,956,958	36	38	723,867	685,769	13,478,479	8.55	7.06
3	Florida	19,893,297	27	29	715,465	666,123	9,946,649	6.31	5.39
4	New York	19,746,227	27	29	724,824	674,837	9,873,114	6.16	5.39
5	Illinois	12,880,580	18	20	715,292	643,763	6,440,290	4.00	3.71
6	Pennsylvania	12,787,209	18	20	709,085	638,177	6,393,605	3.98	3.71
7	Ohio	11,594,163	16	18	721,514	641,346	5,797,082	3.61	3.34
8	Georgia	10,097,343	14	16	708,568	619,997	5,048,672	3.18	2.97
9	North Carolina	9,943,964	13	15	750,159	650,138	4,971,982	3.12	2.79
10	Michigan	9,909,877	14	16	705,954	617,710	4,954,939	3.11	2.97
11	New Jersey	8,938,175	12	14	738,716	633,185	4,469,088	2.79	2.60
12	Virginia	8,326,289	11	13	744,170	629,682	4,163,145	2.61	2.42
13	Washington	7,061,530	10	12	689,701	574,751	3,530,765	2.23	2.23
14	Massachusetts	6,745,408	9	11	738,460	604,195	3,372,704	2.21	2.05
15	Arizona	6,731,484	9	11	728,139	595,750	3,365,742	2.11	2.05
16	Indiana	6,596,855	9	11	726,370	594,303	3,298,428	2.06	2.05
17	Tennessee	6,549,352	9	11	717,360	586,931	3,274,676	2.05	2.05
18	Missouri	6,063,589	8	10	752,749	602,199	3,031,795	1.89	1.86
19	Maryland	5,976,407	8	10	735,570	588,456	2,988,204	1.87	1.86
20	Wisconsin	5,757,564	8	10	715,800	572,640	2,878,782	1.80	1.86
21	Minnesota	5,457,173	8	10	672,392	537,914	2,728,587	1.71	1.86
22	Colorado	5,355,856	7	9	741,083	576,398	2,677,928	1.70	1.67
23	Alabama	4,849,377	7	9	688,860	535,780	2,424,689	1.51	1.67
24	South Carolina	4,832,482	7	9	674,818	524,858	2,416,241	1.52	1.67
25	Louisiana	4,649,676	6	8	766,982	575,237	2,324,838	1.45	1.49
26	Kentucky	4,413,457	6	8	730,069	547,552	2,206,729	1.38	1.49
27	Oregon	3,970,239	5	7	779,871	557,050	1,985,120	1.25	1.30
28	Oklahoma	3,878,051	5	7	762,964	544,974	1,939,026	1.22	1.30

RANK	State	Population	House Seats	Elect. Votes	Pop. per House Seat	Pop. per Elect. Vote	Pop. per Senate Seat	% of Total US Pop	% of Total Elect. Vote
29	Connecticut	3,596,677	5	7	718,059	512,907	1,798,339	1.13	1.30
30	Iowa	3,107,126	4	6	768,547	513,364	1,553,563	0.97	1.12
31	Arkansas	2,994,079	4	6	737,283	491,522	1,497,040	0.93	1.12
32	Mississippi	2,984,926	4	6	746,232	497,488	1,492,463	0.93	1.12
33	Utah	2,942,902	4	6	713,822	475,881	1,471,451	0.93	1.12
34	Kansas	2,904,021	4	6	721,476	480,984	1,452,011	0.91	1.12
35	Nevada	2,839,099	4	6	689,733	459,822	1,419,550	0.90	1.12
36	New Mexico	2,085,572	3	5	695,179	417,108	1,042,786	0.65	0.93
37	Nebraska	1,881,503	3	5	618,508	371,105	940,752	0.59	0.93
38	West Virginia	1,850,326	3	5	618,471	371,083	925,163	0.57	0.93
39	Idaho	1,634,464	2	4	797,864	398,932	817,232	0.51	0.74
40	Hawaii	1,419,561	2	4	696,157	348,078	709,781	0.45	0.74
41	Maine	1,330,089	2	4	664,596	332,298	665,045	0.45	0.74
42	New Hampshire	1,326,813	2	4	660,359	330,180	663,407	0.41	0.74
43	Rhode Island	1,055,173	2	4	525,146	262,273	527,587	0.33	0.74
44	Montana	1,023,579	1	3	1,005,141	335,047	511,790	0.32	0.56
45	Delaware	935,614	1	3	917,092	305,697	467,807	0.29	0.56
46	South Dakota	853,175	1	3	833,354	277,785	426,588	0.27	0.56
47	North Dakota	739,482	1	3	699,628	233,209	369,741	0.24	0.56
48	Alaska	737,732	1	3	736,732	243,816	368,866	0.23	0.56
49	Vermont	626,011	1	3	626,562	208,670	313,006	0.19	0.56
50	Wyoming	584,153	1	3	576,412	192,137	292,077	0.18	0.56

Another shortcoming of the Electoral College is its slowness and untimeliness when it comes to making adjustments to the division of Electoral votes. These changes aimed at reflecting the decline or increase in the population of the different states in the USA take place once every ten years, which is usually after every census. In effect, that means elections held a couple of years between censuses do not truly reflect the changes in the size of the populations of the different states, changes that are expected to be uneven because some states experience higher population growth than others. In fact, California, Florida and Texas account for close to half (48%) of the population growth in the United States of America between 2014 and 2015, even though when the populations of these states are combined, they account for only 27 percent of the US. Population. And with only 22.67 Electoral votes between them in the 2016 Presidential Election, it is fair to say that they got cheated out of about 5 Electoral votes. One can even say that since Donald Trump won in Florida and Texas, two states whose Electoral votes exceeds California's when combined, he did not get a bad deal, especially when talking only about those three states. And Clinton didn't get a bad deal either when taking only these three growth states into account. Now, the combined population of these three states is projected to exceed 100 million by 2030, and would account for about 30 percent of the USA's total. This leaves most pundits wondering whether future changes to the apportioning of Electoral votes are going to take this growth into account.

So, the question looms. Can Americans bet on appropriate adjustments to the Electoral College process in a manner that would reflect the demographic changes these three states are experiencing owing to a combination of factors like natural population growth that is above the national average because of high birth rates among first-generation and second-generation immigrants, and also because of the high domestic and international migration to these warm states due to their good economies among other things?

Population Growth of California, Florida, and Texas

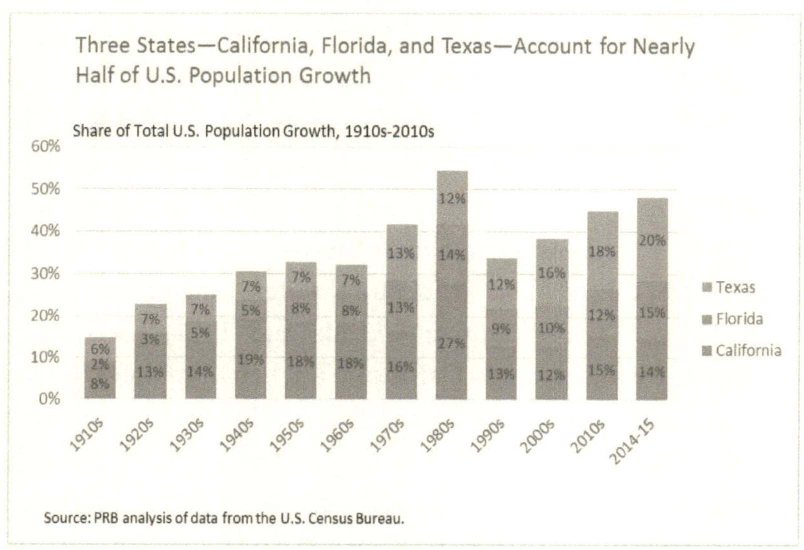

As Americans grapple with the question of the Electoral College process and try to figure out ways to make it effective so that it does not embarrass the country with results that are out of sync with the Popular Vote, we have people who go about looking for answers by first wondering how this two-and-a-half century mechanism came about. So, these questions loom:

- How did the United States of America come to adopt the Electoral College process?
- What is the way forward to make the Electoral College an enriching component of the American Electoral Process, so that it stops playing a

controversial role in the election of future presidents
of the United States of America?

This unique aspect of American democracy came about during the 1787 Constitutional Convention. The delegates were particularly distrustful of the "passions of the people", and strongly believed that the average voter lacked the ability to "wisely" choose a president in a national election, so they came up with the Electoral College—a system that gave each state a number of electors based on the number of members the states get in Congress—one for each member of the House of Representatives plus two for the Senators. The Congress would then set a date during which the state legislatures would select electors, who, on a chosen date, would convene in their respective state capitals to cast their votes for the President and Vice-President of the United States of America.

The Electoral College might have been a practical process back in the eighteenth and early nineteenth century, since there were no political parties at the time for the electors to choose the President and his Vice-President from, a situation that made the whole process seem like a one-party democracy of patriots. All that was expected from these electors were for them to use their best judgment to choose a president and his vice in an atmosphere devoid of partisan politics. And since the electors were people who took pride in their rationality, they made sure they carried out the election in such a patriotic manner that the system looked for a long time like an infallible form of voting. In fact, many pundits today look at the nonpartisan atmosphere at the time as America's golden age of democracy, where the stakeholders believed they had an optimal system that was invaluable in the process of building a great democracy and a great country. But there is an often-unspoken aspect of the nature of the democracy the founding fathers practiced.

The Electoral College was also created with the objective of protecting the interests of southern slaveholders. And since there were people back then who could not turn a blind eye to slavery, among whom were those who were even vehemently opposed to it, the process could not be universally accepted as perfect. Called progressives at the time, these anti-slavery upholders of democracy had misgivings about the Electoral College process and were eventually rewarded in their wishes to see it reformed. That came about with the rise of the two-party system in the nineteenth century.

The two-party system forced the Electoral College to evolve, so that with the exception of Nebraska and Maine, states could choose their electors based on a winner-take-all basis. In the last century, voters did not have to dwell on the merits or the demerits of the Electoral votes because those candidates the American people voted in as president won both the Electoral votes and the Popular Votes. However, things changed right at the start of the twenty-first century when in the 2000 Presidential Election, the Democratic nominee Al Gore won the Popular Vote and lost the Electoral vote to George W. Bush of the Republican Party. So, the fact that it has happened again 16 years after, thereby depriving the America people once again of their chance of making history by voting to power the country's first female president, many Americans, the majority of Americans in fact, do not find it funny anymore.

Still, we have people who continue to defend the Electoral College process, arguing that it provides a check on the public in case the people make an unwise choice for president of the greatest country on earth. They hold onto the rightness of their views even though it is obvious today that party conventions and party leaders choose electors because of their loyalty to their parties and not because of their deep patriotism. And since most Americans do not take this argument seriously anymore because the United States of America is now a country of multi-party politics where electors are no longer seen as independent agents or even as agents of the state legislature, there is a need to decide again on whether to carry out a major reformation of the Electoral College or whether to abolish it altogether.

Nobody disputes the fact that the electors have rarely acted independently and rarely went against the wishes of the party that chose them. There are even laws in most states making it a requirement for the electors to keep their pledges in casting their votes. This explains why over 99 percent of electors kept their pledges to the candidates of their parties in the Presidential Elections between 1992 and 2012.

So, should we have expected some of the Republican Electors not to vote for Donald Trump in the Electoral College process?

- It was highly unlikely since that would have vindicated Donald Trump's claim that the political establishment (the elites of both the Republican and Democratic parties) were against him for malicious reasons that do not serve the interest of America and the average American.

Map of the 2016 Electoral College

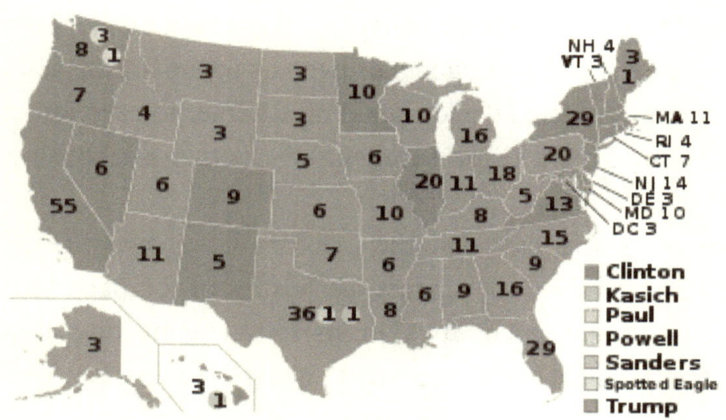

Presidential Election Results map of the Electoral College process held on December 19, 2016.

- Red denotes states Donald Trump and his elected vice president Mike Pence won.
- Blue denotes those states won by Hillary Clinton and his running mate Tim Kaine.
- The other colors represent seven cases where renegades or faithless electors defied the political parties they were representing and cast their votes for others as a sign of protests. These electors were in Texas, Washington, and Hawaii and voted for Colin Powell (3), John Kasich (1), Ron Paul (1), Faith Spotted Eagle (1), or Bernie Sanders (1). Numbers indicate Electoral votes allotted to the winner of each state.

Results of the December 19, 2016 Electoral College Process

State	Party	Presidential vote	Vice presidential vote	Name of Elector
National		Donald Trump 304	Mike Pence 304	Pledged
National		Hillary Clinton 227	Tim Kaine 227	Pledged
Hawaii		Bernie Sanders (I-VT)	Elizabeth Warren (D-MA)	David Mulinix
Texas		John Kasich (R-OH)	one vote (by whom is unknown)	Christopher Suprun
Texas		Ron Paul (L-TX / R-TX)	for Carly Fiorina (R-CA) one vote for Mike Pence	unknown
Washington		Colin Powell (R-VA)[393]	Maria Cantwell (D-WA)	
Washington		Colin Powell (R-VA)	Susan Collins (R-ME)	
Washington		Colin Powell (R-VA)	Elizabeth Warren (D-MA)	
Washington		Faith Spotted Eagle (I-SD)[394]	Winona LaDuke (G-CA / D-CA)	Robert Satiacum Jr.

The fact that there were altogether 7 electors who went rogue in the Electoral College process that ended on December 19, 2016 says a lot about the two major candidates in the 2016 Presidential Election, and gives Americans a better understanding of the depth of division not only within their respective parties, but also in the general society.

The December 19, 2016, Electoral College process stunned Americans with the high number of renegade electors (5 in total) from the Democratic Party:

- From the state of Washington, 3 electors of the Democratic Party chose Collin Powell who is a

Republican, and then split their votes when it came to the position of vice-president, choosing Maria Cantwell (a Democrat from Washington), Elizabeth Warren (a Democrat from Maryland) and Susan Collins (a Republican from Maine).

- Robert Satiacum Jr., a Democratic Party elector from Washington state, took his renegation a step further by choosing for president Faith Spotted Eagle, a female member of the Yankton Sioux Nation who helped block development of the Keystone XL pipeline and the Dakota Access Pipeline. For the position of vice-president, Robert Satiacum Jr. chose Winona LaDuke, an environmentalist of mixed Jewish/Native-American background.

- Democratic elector David Mulinix from Hawaii tried to send home a different message in her choice for the person to represent him as president of the United States of America by casting his vote for Bernie Sanders who lost in the primaries to Hillary Clinton. His vote for Elizabeth Warren, who is also of the Democratic Party, to be Bernie Sander's deputy, gave his protest vote some credulity since Bernie Sanders has a high standing among the left-wingers in the Democratic Party who are still ruing his loss in the primaries.

The 2 rogue or "faithless" electors of the Republican Party that made statements with their votes in the Electoral College process came from Texas. Christopher Suprun and an unknown Republican elector voted for Ohio Republican Gov. John Kasich, who won the third-place in the 2016 Republican primaries, and for Ron Paul who was a candidate in the 2012 Republican Party primaries. They settled for Mike Pence and Carly Fiorina respectively as their choices for vice president of the United States of America.

The 2016 Electoral College process was dramatic all right. But it is understandable, especially when we take into account the unusualness of the primaries, the passion-driven nature of the campaigns ran by Donald Trump and Hillary Clinton, the shocking nature of the election results, and the post-election reactions. So, it is not surprising that the electors cast their votes on December 19, 2016 in an atmosphere permeated by recent media reports accusing Russia and its president Vladimir Putin of hacking and influencing the election, accusations that some pundits construed as a last-ditch attempt by the political establishment to use the Electoral College process to prevent President-elect Donald Trump from being inaugurated on January 20, 2017 as the 45th president of the United States of America. Many people saw it as an attempt to convince electors of both parties from casting their votes against the President-elect.

It is obvious most Americans do not like it, but the fact that the Electoral College system produced two controversial elections within two decades—2000 and 2016, says something about a need to look into its effectiveness. It is understandable then why there is a widespread call from Democrats this time around, asking for its abolition without delay. This call is not likely to get a major resistance because it would be difficult for anyone to raise a logical argument against it at this point in time.

In fact, even Republicans and nonpartisan Americans agree that the rationality or irrationality of the Electoral College process distorts the presidential campaigns as it discourages candidates and their parties from campaigning in all the states of the country, and as it discourages them from campaigning in both the rural and the urban areas nationwide. A deep analysis of the campaigns reveals that the Republican and Democratic presidential candidates have been writing off the more than 40 states that they either find unwinnable or impossible to lose, leaving behind a situation where it is virtually accepted by almost everyone that most states today are either traditional Republican or traditional Democratic. Just about ten states are considered swing states and less than half of them, such as Florida, Ohio, North Carolina, Virginia etc., have become traditional swing states.

Today, these swing states are the focus of campaigns and are viewed as the states to please, especially when it comes to presidents who are seeking reelection. That leaves major states like California, Texas, New York etc. in the cold owing to the simple fact that their colors tend to be determined well in advance of elections. The irony is that these traditional Republican Party and traditional Democratic Party states tend to be among the highest financial contributors to the campaign funds in all the elections, yet they hardly get any of the money plowed back into their economies as campaign expenditures made in their states.

The merits and demerits of the Electoral College speak for themselves, but the peculiar thing about this process is that Donald Trump will emerge from it with a stronger mandate to govern than he would have had, had he been the winning candidate in a close Electoral vote and a close Popular Vote against the Democratic candidate Hillary Clinton.

CHAPTER FIVE

Economy & Declining Income

Voters and their Household Income Range

Demographic	Household income					
	Under $30k	$30k–$50k	$50k–$100k	$100k–$200k	$200k–$250k	$250k or more
Trump	41%	42%	50%	48%	49%	48%
Clinton	53%	51%	46%	47%	48%	46%

The United States of America has been through a period of roughly thirty years of economic growth bedeviled with increasing poverty and a decline of the middle class, where most of the population has been left out of the economic expansion and development. During this period, which has been spearheaded by globalization that has produced the greatest growth of wealth in the history of humanity, there have been winners and losers. And even though the gains made by the US. economy are much higher than in previous generations, only a small portion of the population benefitted from the windfall, which explains why there has been this phenomenal rise in the number of billionaires and millionaires. For most Americans, their wages either stagnated or declined during this period, which is why many are questioning the benefits of the much-touted globalization and fair trade.

In a nutshell, the changes experienced by the US. economy during the past fifty years has been big. Unfortunately, it has not led to an improvement in the standard of living of most Americans, a failure that affected White Americans the most. It is this demographic group that experienced a higher decline in their level of income and standard of living than the other racial groups, so that the 5.2% rise in Median Income in 2015 could not dent the pent-up anger most of them were already having, a rancor that has always been directed at the political establishment.

One would expect concerted efforts by those left behind to come up with an organized resistance to the developments taking place in the economy; one would have expected non-mainstream figures with thought formulations that are clear and valid to be the ones challenging the political establishment responsible for this growing economic and social disparity. But that has not been the case. In fact, much of what Americans experienced in the past were protests, and much of the protests were scattered, short-lived and not widespread. But then the 2016 race for the White House brought forth Donald Trump and Bernie Sanders, two mavericks from opposite ends of the economic, political and ideological spectrums, who successfully tapped the dissatisfaction of most Americans and made the majority of these struggling people, who feel that they have been left behind due to the machinations of a rigged system, believe that they could challenge what some have been regarding over the years as an unshakable corporatocracy. This new belief in the ability of the common folk of America to force the political establishment to carry out changes that would benefit all the citizens of the USA got transformed into a generalized rage during the election campaigns. In fact, the rage was seen in all the groups in America. White Americans, especially White males, expressed this rage the most and in a targeted manner, so that they voted to power the man who understand their rage the most and tapped it in such a manner that they did not feel they were being taken advantage of.

As a matter of fact, when Donald Trump kicked off his bid for the presidency and when he started sparring with the other sixteen Republican aspirants in the primaries, many Americans viewed him as a clown who would be fettered and rendered irrelevant. But he proved his detractors wrong. He evolved all right, but he did not shake off his clownish approach, which with the ordinariness of the other Republican candidates, made the Republican primaries interesting not for their substantiated content, but for their failures to address pertinent issues. In fact, none of the candidates came out with policies that were clearly spelled out. Yet Donald Trump distinguished himself from his Republican competitors, emerged as the winner, and then went on to win the Presidential Election on the back of the substantive support he got from mostly White Americans, a phenomenon CNN's political commentator called "White lash" on the night of November 8, 2016, after it dawned on him that Donald Trump had just won the Presidential Election.

Filmmaker Michael Moore was even more insightful and framed it a lot better when hardly a month before election day, he told a group of CNBC panelists that Donald Trump's supporters see the Republican nominee "as their human Molotov cocktail…not because they agree with him…but because of the opportunity to use him, to just whip him into the system and blow it up." He was right. Some would say that Van Jones was right too.

When we pry deeper into why Donald Trump pulled off the biggest upset in the history of Presidential Elections in the United States of America, we can see that in his so-called clownish ways, he courted support from the electorate in a strategic manner that could be considered ingenious. Yes, on November 08, 2016, a lot of White Americans from poor, working class, middle-class backgrounds etc., White Americans of mostly of traditional families who were not happy with the socio-economic and political direction the country was taking, voted the billionaire and political novice to power in key states that determined he won the Electoral vote over Hillary Clinton, the Democratic nominee that almost everyone thought was going to win. Donald Trump, the maverick outsider in the 2016 Presidential Election won by appealing to the feelings of dissatisfied voters. He did so by tapping their grievances in a manner that had not been seen before, and he carried out his engagement with these people in strategic states that most Democratic Party strategists took for granted or didn't pay enough attention to.

The leadership in the US. political establishment cannot be accused of not having the gut-level grasp of the mood in the country, especially among minorities and those left behind by economic developments in the country over the past three decades. But what they can be accused of is for failing to respond appropriately to the growing distress caused by their internal policies and the workings of the international market. In fact, while the number of Americans in the lower class has been increasing over the years, the rate of decrease in income and/or increase in the rate of poverty has been highest among White Americans than among other racial groups in the country. And this has been mostly in the Southeast and the Rustbelt (areas of the Northeastern and Midwestern US that are characterized by declining industries, aging factories, and a falling population) —which begins in the state of New York and stretches westward through Pennsylvania, West Virginia, Ohio, Indiana, the Lower Peninsula of Michigan, and ending in northern Illinois, eastern Iowa, and southeastern Wisconsin.

However, it is particularly in the Rustbelt—the part of the American Midwest that for decades voted the Democratic Party due to the special alliance forged between organized labor and the Democratic Party since the Great Depression, an alliance that persists today, though in a moribund state due to the deindustrialization that has been going on in the area for the past three decades—that Donald dealt a death-blow to Hillary Clinton, the Democratic Party and the political establishment as a whole. In this part of the country that not long ago was the cradle of the middle class, but which is now haunted by shuttered factories, crumbling roads and bridges, hollowed out downtowns, crime-ridden and dying cities, Donald Trump and his campaign successfully galvanized former members and supporters of the Democratic Party and organized labor, and then convinced them and won their votes in the 2016 election. This departure of former members of organized labor and the Democratic Party to the Trump camp, and maybe to the Republican Party, may end up as a permanent divorce between these Midwestern states and the Democratic Party. Worthy of special note is the fact that Catholicism is dominant in these Rustbelt States. Cognizance should also be taken of the fact that the Germanic (ethnic Germans, ethnic Dutch, and Scandinavians) populations form the absolute majority in these Rustbelt states.

While the Rustbelt happens to encompass states that are especially known for their tradition of voting Democrats, the Southeast has traditionally voted Republican. All Donald Trump needed to do in these Southeastern states was to consolidate their vote. And he did a brilliant job doing that, so that even the wavering North Carolina that voted the Democratic Party candidate Barack Obama in the 2008 Presidential Election, voted Republican in 2016.

It is true most of Donald Trump's supporters were angry, but they had every reason to be. After all, they were the group affected the most by:

- the loss of homes due to foreclosures following the 2008 recession,
- the loss of jobs due to the transfer of manufacturing jobs overseas or abroad, and the loss of jobs due to the effects of the recession,
- stagnation in the minimum wage due to the availability of cheap labor provided by both legal and illegal immigrants,
- rising professionalism, increasing automation and the growing technological orientation of the American economy, changes that are taking place mostly in urban areas known for harboring most of America's minority racial groups, hence making it possible for a higher proportion of these minorities to become more adaptive to the changing economy than most White Americans who abound mostly in the suburbs, countryside and small towns of rural America.

Median Household Income by State

Rank	State	2014	2010	2009	2007	2000
1	Maryland	$70,004	$69,272	$70,545	$87,080	$72,372
2	New Jersey	$69,825	$68,342	$70,378	$84,035	$70,169
3	California	$67,458	$67,034	$71,595	$90,967	$81,972
4	Connecticut	$65,753	$66,953	$68,460	$81,333	$67,639
	District of Columbia	$65,124	$63,098	$57,214	$52,746	$50,681
5	Massachusetts	$64,859	$62,081	$61,401	$59,365	$56,236
6	New Hampshire	$64,712	$63,557	$62,731	$61,369	$60,489
7	Virginia	$62,881	$61,330	$58,233	$59,562	$55,108
8	Hawaii	$62,814	$59,290	$57,936	$97,317	[1]

Rank	State	2014	2010	2009	2007	2000
9	Minnesota	$61,814	$58,931	$57,021	$59,948	$53,770
10	Alaska	$60,287	$69,860	$79,989	$95,470	$90,214
11	Delaware	$57,954	$58,548	$60,078	$85,591	$73,439
12	Washington	$57,835	$54,616	$52,288	$50,082	$50,011
13	Wyoming	$56,322	$55,430	$56,993	$55,212	$54,039
14	Utah	$55,869	$55,117	$56,633	$55,109	$55,179
15	Colorado	$55,387	$54,659	$56,033	$53,514	$48,201
16	New York	$55,246	$54,119	$55,701	$53,914	$52,003
17	Rhode Island	$53,636	$53,966	$56,235	$54,124	$49,280
18	Illinois	$53,234	$53,341	$56,361	$55,062	$50,819
19	Vermont	$52,776	$52,664	$53,207	$51,731	$47,227

Rank	State	2014	2010	2009	2007	2000
20	North Dakota	$51,704	$51,618	$52,104	$49,907	$51,622
	United States	$50,502	$50,221	$52,029	$50,740	-
21	Wisconsin	$50,395	$49,993	$52,094	$50,578	$48,874
22	Nebraska	$50,296	$49,520	$50,713	$48,576	$47,791
23	Pennsylvania	$50,228	$48,745	$50,958	$49,889	$46,729
24	Iowa	$49,427	$48,457	$50,169	$48,730	$45,485
25	Texas	$49,392	$48,259	$50,043	$47,548	$43,425
26	Kansas	$48,964	$48,044	$48,980	$47,292	$47,489
27	Nevada	$48,927	$47,827	$45,685	$43,753	$43,753
28	South Dakota	$48,321	$47,817	$50,177	$47,451	$44,264
29	Oregon	$46,816	$47,590	$50,861	$49,136	$46,841

Rank	State	2014	2010	2009	2007	2000
30	Arizona	$46,709	$47,357	$49,693	$47,085	$48,126
31	Indiana	$46,438	$45,734	$46,581	$45,888	$45,040
32	Maine	$46,033	$45,424	$47,966	$47,448	$44,806
33	Georgia	$46,007	$45,395	$47,988	$46,597	$45,837
34	Michigan	$45,981	$45,255	$48,591	$47,950	$47,064
35	Ohio	$45,749	$45,229	$46,867	$45,114	$44,651
36	Missouri	$45,247	$45,043	$46,032	$43,424	$44,624
37	Florida	$44,299	$44,926	$47,576	$46,253	$46,395
38	Montana	$44,222	$44,736	$47,778	$47,804	$44,448
39	North Carolina	$43,916	$43,674	$46,549	$44,670	$42,061
40	Idaho	$43,341	$43,028	$43,508	$41,452	$40,827

Rank	State	2014	2010	2009	2007	2000
41	Oklahoma	$43,225	$42,492	$43,733	$40,926	$37,943
42	South Carolina	$42,367	$42,442	$44,625	$43,329	$40,822
43	New Mexico	$41,963	$42,322	$43,654	$43,531	$38,629
44	Louisiana	$41,734	$41,725	$43,614	$42,367	$40,676
45	Tennessee	$41,693	$41,664	$42,822	$41,567	$40,001
46	Alabama	$41,415	$40,489	$42,666	$40,554	$38,473
47	Kentucky	$41,141	$40,072	$41,538	$40,267	$38,466
	Guam	$38,973	-	-	-	-
48	Arkansas	$38,758	$37,823	$38,815	$38,134	$37,420
49	West Virginia	$38,482	$37,435	$37,989	$37,060	$37,227
50	Mississippi	$36,919	$36,646	$37,790	$36,338	$35,261

Rank	State	2014	2010	2009	2007	2000
	U.S. Virgin Islands	$30,921	-	-	-	-
	Northern Mariana Islands	$23,171	-	-	-	-
	Puerto Rico	$23,168	-	-	-	-
	American Samoa	-	$34,254 [3]	-	-	$17,018 [4]

Now, we have a clearer picture of why most White Americans, especially those white males who still feel that everything has been taken away from them, used Donald Trump as their proverbial "Human Molotov Cocktail", per Michael Moore. They were truly furious about everything. They blame the system or the institutions, more especially the last two presidencies—they fault the previous President George W. Bush, the brother of John Ellis "Jeb" Bush Sr. whom they rejected in the primaries in a resounding manner in favor of Donald Trump; they hold the administration of the outgoing President Barack Obama responsible as well—for working against them in favor of the privileged minority in the country, the club of millionaires and billionaires as many like to call these economic elites.

It is not an understatement to say that a substantial portion of what the mainstream media dubbed "Angry White Americans" who voted for Donald Trump felt deeply that they were losing their country because "the elites" were taking it away from them. And to them, the millionaire Hillary Clinton stood as the poster child of the political establishment far more than the billionaire Donald Trump. After all, didn't Donald Trump prove earlier that he had what it takes to turn the Rustbelt around during a Detroit Economic Club meeting where he spelt it out to Ford Motor executives in no uncertain terms that their plan to close factories in Detroit, Michigan and move them to Mexico, would be met by a 35% tax on the Ford cars that would be manufactured in the Latin-American country, and then shipped back to the United States of America, which would make them overpriced in the USA for anybody to buy? Yes, Donald Trump said that, and it was an amazing feat and music to the ears of the people of the Rustbelt states of Michigan, Ohio, Pennsylvania, and Wisconsin.

No politician of the Republican Party or the Democratic Party ever confronted executives of Corporate America in such a fearless manner before. And apparently, the Ford Motor executives blinked. They budged all right and the factories they were planning to move to Mexico are going to stay in the states they are located in for the foreseeable future. In fact, reports from CNN and other mainstream media confirmed Ford's press report on January 04, 2017 stating that the Ford Automobile company had just cancelled plans to build a $1.6 billion factory in Mexico, and that the company would invest $700 million in Michigan instead, which would result in the creation of 700 new U.S. jobs. As if to vindicate the Michigan population for voting Donald Trump to power, Ford's CEO Mark Fields stated that the investment is a "vote of confidence" in the pro-business environment that Donald

Trump created in the country.

The Ford case shows that the president-elect kept up his pressure on Ford Automobile, and in a way, it paid off in the long run since the $700 million that Ford is going to invest will go to the Flat Rock plant in Michigan, for the purpose of producing more electric and self-driving cars. The fact that the Ford CEO told CNN's Poppy Harlow in an exclusive interview that: "We didn't cut a deal with Trump. We did it for our business.", goes to confirm the new view that Ford is convinced electrified vehicles are going to outsell gas-powered vehicles within the next 15 years, and so wants to lead in that direction.

The Ford turn around and the fact that the president-elect has accomplished a similar feat with Carrier, the Farmington, Connecticut-based brand of United Technologies Corporation Building & Industrial Systems, which is involved in manufacturing and distributing heating, ventilating and air conditioning (HVAC) systems, as well as commercial refrigeration and food service equipment, reflects the growing business confidence in the country and the positive expectation businesses have of Donald Trump when he gets sworn in as the 45th president of the United States of America on January 20, 2017. He has just saved 1,100 jobs that Carrier was about to move to Mexico.

True Trump's opponents claim the early December deal with Carrier involved tax incentives to the company as an enticement for it to stay put in the USA, which in their opinion is a bad way of saving jobs. However, to those whose jobs have been saved, and to Trump's supporters in particular, the opponents of the Carrier deal are nothing more than detractors that harbor ill-feelings against a man who is an effective deal-maker with the proven leadership skills to turn things around even in near-impossible situations like in the cases of the Ford and the Carrier corporations.

The Major Industries in the States of the USA

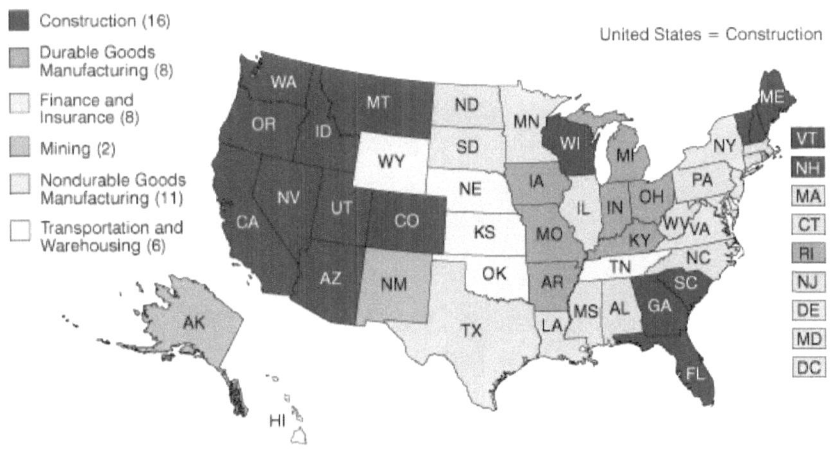

GDP Per Capita of States in the USA

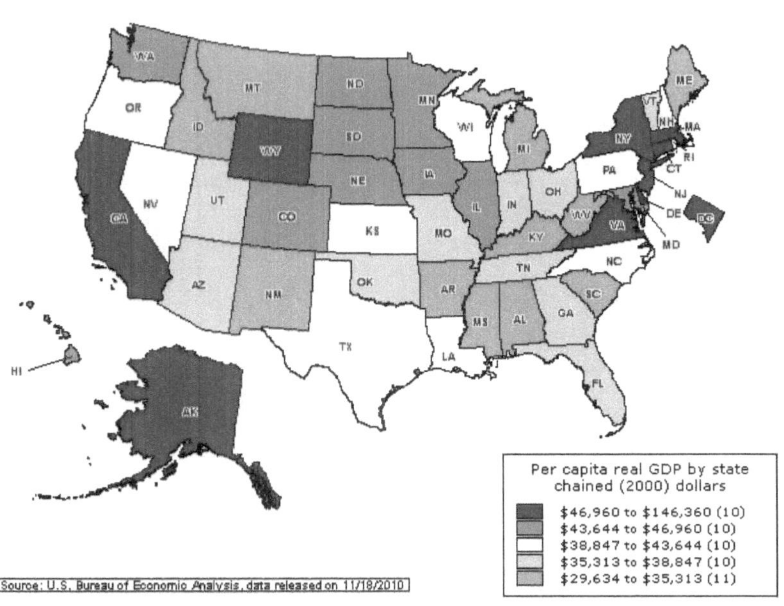

US. GDP Per Capita

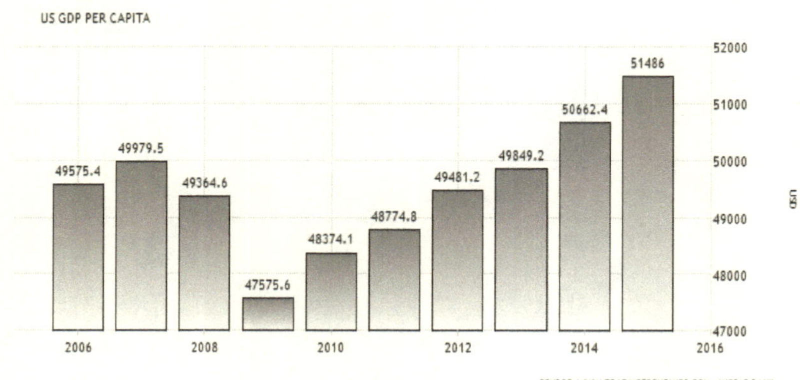

GDP Growth by State, 2015: IV-2016: I

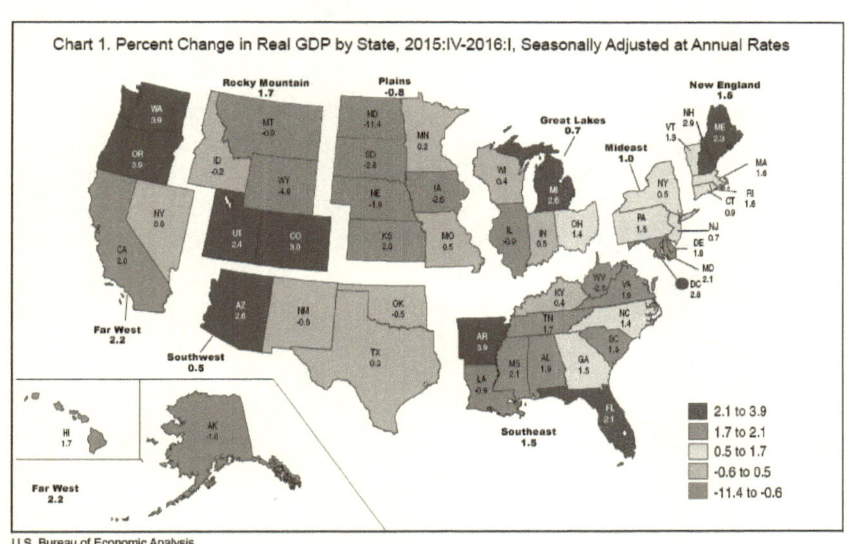

U.S. Bureau of Economic Analysis

Yes, Donald Trump promised transformative changes to America's shrinking middle class and his words were deeply taken to heart by the voters of the Rustbelt states, the part of the country where the middle class got hit the hardest by the 2008 recession that began under the presidency of George Bush. Barack Obama tried his best to revive this middle class, but it wasn't enough, especially in these Rustbelt states.

Donald Trump's galvanization of underprivileged White Americans, especially in the Southeast and Rustbelt, White Americans who think that "They have been cut off from the American Pie", White Americans who are mostly non-Anglo-Saxon or are not of English descent, contributed enormously to his strength in winning this election. And based on how things turn out in the next four years, this group of the electorate will come in handy in the next presidential election in 2020. Donald Trump can count on their future loyalty because he has successfully he has brought with him a new base into the political map of the country, a base of poor White Americans who decades ago worked in states that were driving the American economy forward, poor White Americans who have seen deindustrialization reduce their economic strength and political importance in the past decades, so that many of them withdrew from America's electoral process, convinced that their voices were not being heard.

Now, these underprivileged voters of the Rustbelt and Southeast feel their votes made a difference in the 2016 Presidential Election and brought Donald Trump to power, a brazen fellow who has promised to shatter any illusions the political establishment could still be having of maintaining the status quo; they feel their votes will make a difference in future elections; they feel Donald Trump will not betray them like the elites of the establishment did before. After all, these elites who ruined their lives hate Donald Trump too; after all Corporate America that let them down hates the maverick billionaire; after all, Wall Street that triggered the 2008 recession looks down on Donald Trump too. So, the man who is about to become the 45th president of the United States of America will always need their votes not only in his fight against the corporatocracy, but also against the career politicians and the mainstream media that loved him before, made a celebrity out of him, and then turned around and now hates him.

The biggest development from the 2016 Presidential Election is the fact that these newly-empowered voters who carried Donald Trump into the White House with their votes do not intend to fall back into the state of political lethargy that for decades convinced politicians to write them off so easily. Now they are relevant and their relevancy would be sought by politicians in future campaigns. Their performance has shown that voters, irrespective of the states they are in, should not be taken for granted. Their brethren in other states are likely to revolt too, increasing the number of swing states, so that future campaigns will become nationwide and make future elections a lot more competitive and difficult to predict. The era of the traditional swing states is over. Many more states are going to be up for grasp, and the new reality could be that the era of traditional Democratic Party states and traditional Republican Party states could be over for all we know.

The Swing States of the 2016 Presidential Election

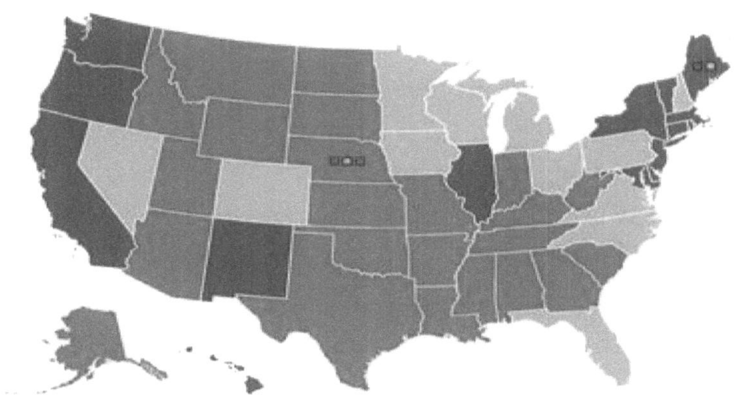

Margin of victory of States in Presidential Elections (1992-2008)

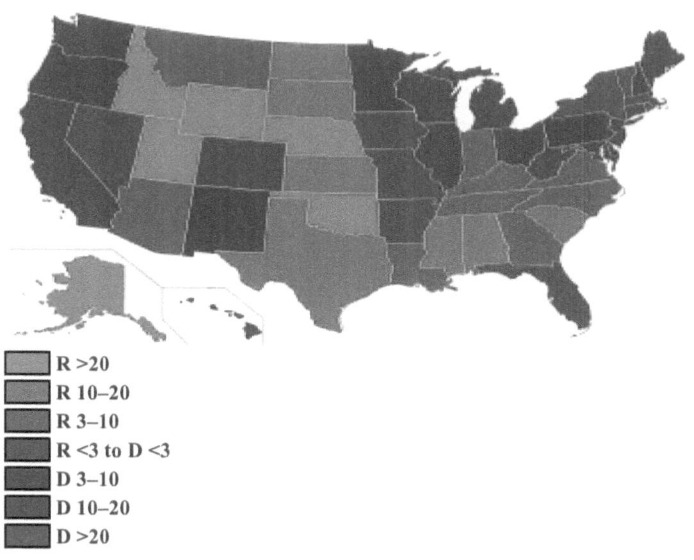

The blue states are traditionally safe for the Democratic Party; the red states are traditionally safe for the Republican Party, and grey states are traditionally regarded as the swing states.

Now, there are enough facts to back up the new reality—a swell in the number of swing states. This new development means that the deciders of future elections will comprise the following states: Colorado, Florida, Georgia, Iowa, Kentucky, Louisiana, Michigan, Minnesota, Montana, New Hampshire, Nevada, North Carolina, Ohio, Pennsylvania, Tennessee, Utah, Virginia, and Wisconsin. The expansion in the number of swing states promises the people robust political campaigns that will illuminate the American political scene for decades to come and that will force the established political parties to either adapt or be made less relevant by new political forces that will fill the vacuum in the years to come.

CHAPTER SIX

Religion

Religious affiliation in the USA (2014)—Pew Research Center Data

Affiliation	% of U.S. population	
Christian	70.6	
Protestant	46.5	
Evangelical Protestant	25.4	
Mainline Protestant	14.7	

Religious affiliation in the USA (2014)—Pew Research Center Data

Affiliation	% of U.S. population	
Black church	6.5	
Catholic	20.8	
Mormon	1.6	
Jehovah's Witnesses	0.8	
Eastern Orthodox	0.5	
Other Christian	0.4	
Unaffiliated	22.8	
Nothing in particular	15.8	
Agnostic	4.0	

Religious affiliation in the USA (2014)—Pew Research Center Data

Affiliation	% of U.S. population	
Atheist	**3.1**	
Non-Christian faiths	**5.9**	
Jewish	**1.9**	
Muslim	**0.9**	
Buddhist	**0.7**	
Hindu	**0.7**	
Other Non-Christian faiths	**1.8**	
Don't know/refused answer	**0.6**	
Total	100	

Map of the Largest Religious Groups in the Different States

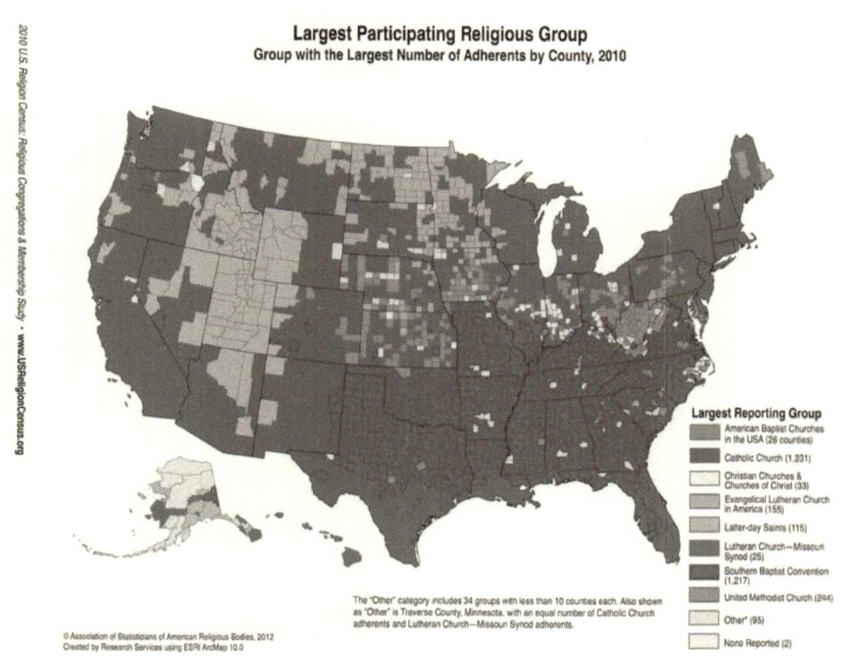

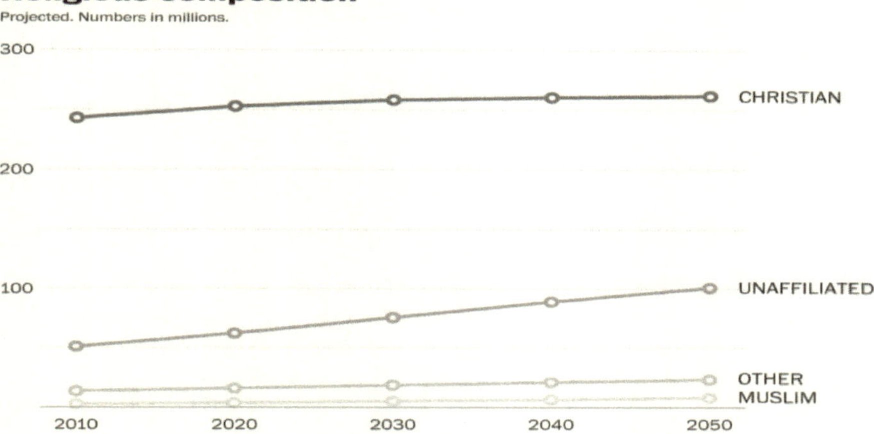

One factor that was particularly overlooked by the Republican campaign in the 2016 US. Presidential race for the White House was the force of sectarianism. Most of the pundits, newsmen, newswomen, and scholars who skimped when it came to talking about the influence of religion in the campaigns could be excused for their oversight because religion never played a major role in past elections, and because all the candidates were from the mainstream Christian denominations. Except for the 2012 Republican Party nominee Mitch Romney who was a Mormon, it was always business as usual. In fact, the media always dwelled on the long-held mantra of Evangelicals and most Protestants voting Republicans, and Catholics voting Democrats. But it turned out not to be the case in the 2016 Presidential Election. Donald Trump the Lutheran courted Catholics with an uncommon zeal that many pundits noticed but only a few dwelled on. Perhaps his mother's Scottish/Free Church of Scotland/Catholic background had something to do with it. All the same, he won their votes. And he won them big in the states that mattered the most in the election—the Rustbelt states. The statistics below bear out all the facts.

Presidential Vote by Religious Affiliation and Race

	2000		2004		2008		2012		Dem change 08-12
	Gore	Bush	Kerry	Bush	Obama	McCain	Obama	Romney	
	%	%	%	%	%	%	%	%	
TOTAL	48	48	48	51	53	46	50	48	-3
Protestant/Other Christian	42	56	40	59	45	54	42	57	-3
White Prot/Other Christian	35	63	32	67	34	65	30	69	-4
Born-again/evangelical	n/a	n/a	21	79	26	73	20	79	-6
Non-evangelical	n/a	n/a	44	55	44	55	44	54	--
Black Prot/Other Christian	92	7	86	13	94	4	95	5	+1
Catholic	50	47	47	52	54	45	50	48	-4
White Catholic	45	52	43	56	47	52	40	59	-7
Hispanic Catholic	65	33	65	33	72	26	75	21	+3
Jewish	79	19	74	25	78	21	69	30	-9
Other faiths	62	28	74	23	73	22	74	23	+1
Religiously unaffiliated	61	30	67	31	75	23	70	26	-5
Mormon	n/a	n/a	19	80	n/a	n/a	21	78	n/a

Note: Throughout this report, "Protestant" refers to people who described themselves as "Protestant," "Mormon" or "other Christian" in exit polls; this categorization most closely approximates the exit poll data reported immediately after the election by media sources.

Note: In this report, a few estimates for 2000, 2004 and 2008 differ slightly from previous Pew Forum analyses due to differences in data coding.

Source: 2004 Hispanic Catholic estimates come from aggregated state exit polls conducted by the National Election Pool. Other estimates come from Voter News Service/National Election Pool national exit polls. 2012 data from NBCNews.com and National Public Radio.

PEW RESEARCH CENTER

Votes by Religion

Candidates	Religion				
	Protestant	Catholic	Jewish	Other	Atheist
Trump	58%	52%	24%	29%	26%
Clinton	39%	45%	71%	62%	68%

Donald trump's earnest serenading of Catholics became glaring during the Alfred E. Smith Memorial Foundation dinner—an annual charity event that has long been a bastion of civility in an otherwise partisan political world. When he remarked to the participants gathered there that "Here she is tonight, in public, pretending not to hate Catholics," it might have been construed by some of the targeted audiences there that night as a passing comment aimed at Hillary Clinton, coming from a man regarded by some as a loose cannon. But the curious thing is that the pronouncement from the then Republican Party's presidential nominee drew jeers from some of those attending this traditionally lighthearted event. In fact, Cardinal Timothy Dolan, the redoubtable archbishop of New York, showed visible signs of unease about the comment. It is hard to imagine that he did not wonder at the time whether his assertion four years ago, that "The purpose of the Al Smith Dinner is to show both our country and our Church at their best", made sense that night. But he looked relaxed after Donald Trump became gracious with his subsequent remarks, and especially after Hillary Clinton took the rostrum and threw back some light-hearted jabs at her Republican rival. One can say that despite the moments of discomfort experienced by some of the participants, the night ended well for all.

As a matter of fact, nobody is harboring any thoughts of seeing the Alfred E. Smith Memorial Foundation cease its longstanding election-year tradition of inviting the presidential candidates of the Republican and the Democratic parties to the white-tie gala, where they would have the opportunity to rub shoulders with other famous and celebrated figures, give their lighthearted speeches, and tease one another and themselves in a good-natured way in the spirit of Alfred E. Smith, the former governor of New York and the first Catholic presidential nominee in the history of the United

States of America.

As we look back at that night in a candid manner, it becomes obvious from the comment the Lutheran/Catholic Donald Trump made that he was reminding Catholic voters he was one of their own, an underdog running against a non-Catholic Hillary Clinton of the United Methodist Church. If not, then what explanation can one give when we know that Lutherans and United Methodists are members of the Mainline Protestant group. Or perhaps he was making a point for his running mate Michael Richard "Mike" Pence who considers himself an Evangelical Catholic, meaning he is a conservative Catholic. And perhaps he thought that the liberal crowd there that night might back Hillary Clinton's running mate Timothy Michael "Tim" Kaine, who is a known progressive Catholic with an old-school, social-justice, Jesuit-trained Catholicism that is more appealing to the voting population in the center of American politics, the group otherwise known as Moderates. If Tim Kaine, was the target, then it also worked because the majority of moderates in the USA voted for Donald Trump.

The Republican Party nominee had every reason to be concerned. The Democratic Party won the majority of Catholic votes in past Presidential Elections, except for the 2004 Presidential Election when John Forbes Kerry, the Democratic Presidential nominee, lost the Catholic vote to the Methodist George W. Bush. Some pundits have attributed Kerry's 2004 loss of the Catholic vote to the Jewish faith of his running mate Joseph Isadore "Joe" Lieberman. To prove to skeptics that the Republican win in 2004 was not a fluke, the Trump campaign decided not to take any chances this time. So, the Alfred E. Smith Memorial Foundation dinner became the occasion to use to transform the split of Catholic votes between Republicans and Democrats in the 2012 Presidential Election into a win of the Catholic vote for

Republicans in 2016. And since Donald Trump believed he would have the election if many Catholics who voted for the Democratic presidential candidate and incumbent Barack Obama in the last elections changed their minds this time and vote for him, just as they would have voted for Alfred E. Smith, the disingenuous remark that Hillary Clinton hated Catholics, turned out to be well orchestrated. This gimmick certainly swayed many Catholic voters that were inclined towards the Democratic Party in the past, to vote for Donald Trump, a factor that contributed in a major way to his victory in Catholic-majority states like Florida and in some of the Catholic-dominated states of the Great Lakes (Wisconsin, Michigan, Ohio, Pennsylvania, Wisconsin) region.

Donald Trump's win of the Catholic vote has set the base for an uneasy alliance between Lutherans, Catholics, and Evangelicals in the Rustbelt and the Southeast (the first and second most popular Christian religious denominations there), especially now that the three denominations agree on many issues. And since mainstream Evangelicalism is strongest in most of the southern states that have always voted Republican, a partnership between Evangelical and Catholic and other Mainline Protestant voters that made Republicans victorious in the wavering southern state of North Carolina where Catholicism is the leading denomination, will make the state permanently Republican in many future Presidential Elections. In fact, this unwritten alliance of the three may even see Virginia turning redder in future presidential elections.

Weekly church attendance by State in 2014

Rank	State	Percent
1	Utah	51%
2	Mississippi	47%
3	Alabama	46%
4	Louisiana	46%
5	Arkansas	45%
6	South Carolina	42%
7	Tennessee	42%
8	Kentucky	41%
9	North Carolina	40%

Weekly church attendance by State in 2014

Rank	State	Percent
10	Georgia	39%
11	Texas	39%
12	Oklahoma	39%
13	New Mexico	36%
14	Nebraska	35%
15	Indiana	35%
16	Virginia	35%
17	Delaware	35%
18	Missouri	35%

Weekly church attendance by State in 2014

Rank	State	Percent
19	Idaho	34%
20	West Virginia	34%
21	Arizona	33%
22	Kansas	33%
23	Michigan	32%
24	Ohio	32%
25	Illinois	32%
26	North Dakota	32%
27	Pennsylvania	32%

Weekly church attendance by State in 2014

Rank	State	Percent
28	Iowa	32%
29	Florida	32%
30	Maryland	31%
31	South Dakota	31%
32	Minnesota	31%
33	New Jersey	30%
34	Wisconsin	29%
35	Rhode Island	28%
36	Wyoming	28%

Weekly church attendance by State in 2014

Rank	State	Percent
37	California	28%
38	New York	27%
39	Nevada	27%
40	Montana	27%
41	Alaska	26%
42	Connecticut	25%
43	Colorado	25%
44	Hawaii	25%
45	Oregon	24%

Weekly church attendance by State in 2014

Rank	State	Percent
46	Washington	24%
47	District of Columbia	23%
48	Massachusetts	22%
49	Maine	20%
50	New Hampshire	20%
51	Vermont	17%

The Trump campaign also counted on the fact that those states with high weekly church attendance where the denominations that dominate vote the candidates identifying with the dominant denominations, would work in their favor since weekly church attendance rates are highest among Conservatives than among Moderates and Liberals. And as has always been the case, most Conservatives vote Republican. That is why it came as no surprise that the predictions made from the data below on weekly church attendance correlate with the results of past elections, especially the recent 2016 vote.

In short, statistics have been consistent in showing us that states where Evangelical Protestants, Conservative Catholics, and Conservative Mainline Protestants dominate, and where weekly church attendance is high, rarely failed to vote Republican. And since Evangelicals and Catholics are the fastest growing denominations in the country, the votes of this set of Christian faithful will be highly coveted and courted by both the Republican and the Democratic parties in future elections.

CHAPTER SEVEN

Globalization and States that Lost Jobs from it

Donald Trump's message of "Making America Great Again" and his promise to bring jobs and manufacturing back to America resonated well in States that lost jobs during the past decades and that saw their manufacturing base shrink not as a result of natural means (increasing unemployment due to companies that folded or shredded workers), but because of conscious business decisions made by the executives of those large corporations who moved parts, most or all of their manufacturing abroad as a result of strategic decisions made by management to cut the cost of production, increase revenue and the profit margin of their companies, and secure foreign markets and/or increase their market share in the foreign countries.

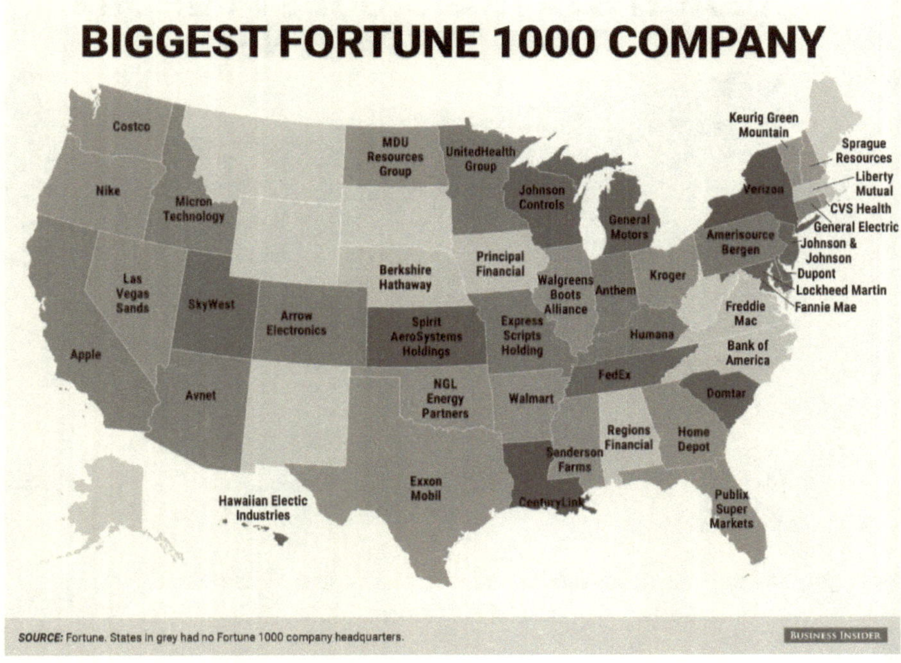

Some of the major consequences of these transfer of jobs abroad owing to the globalization trend that is characterized by fair trade, have been a shrinking middle class in the affected states, the decline in unionization and membership in trade unions, population decline, and high unemployment in those states that saw their jobs transferred abroad. However, it is the high level of unemployment with its attendant problems of alcoholism, drug abuse, crime and disease in the former manufacturing areas and in those states that witnessed deindustrialization, that fuels the grievances of these affected Americans who feel like the rug has been pulled from under their feet, and are therefore resentful of their fallen status. China, which benefitted more than any other country from this job and technology transfers, is today the world's leading manufacturing country. This US-led Western transfer of capital and manufacturing to the quasi-Communist Asian giant ended up benefitting China, the Chinese people, and the top 1% of America and the rest of the Western World, but it failed to improve the wellbeing of the common folk of the industrialized countries of the West, especially the middle class of these countries.

This deindustrialization in the USA, coupled with the flood of goods from China, leave a sour taste in the mouths of underprivileged Americans, especially the former industrial workers and their families in these former manufacturing areas. This phenomenon is felt most acutely in the Rustbelt where the people are deeply convinced that the principal concerns of the political establishment and the past US. governments are the interests and welfare of the elites of the country who see globalization as the best way for them to increase their wealth multiple folds.

Growth of GDP and Household Income

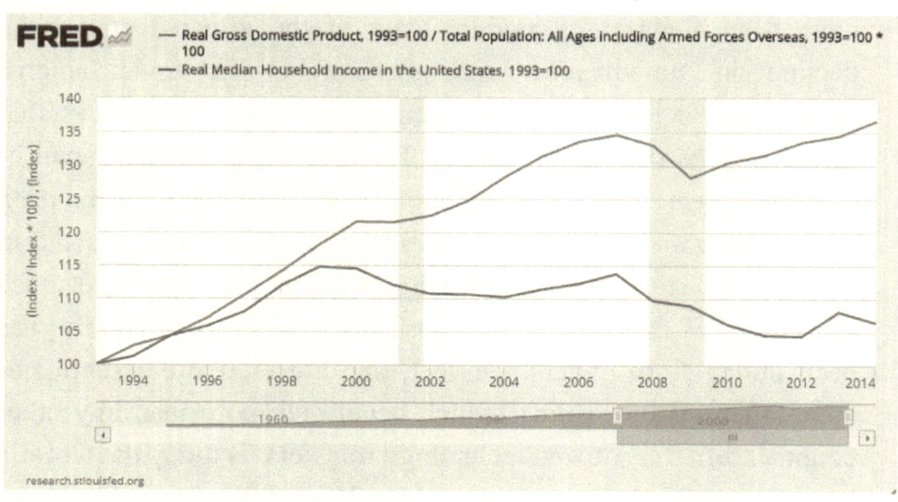

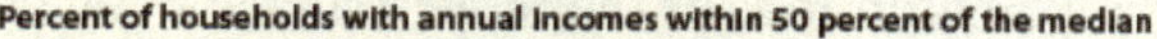

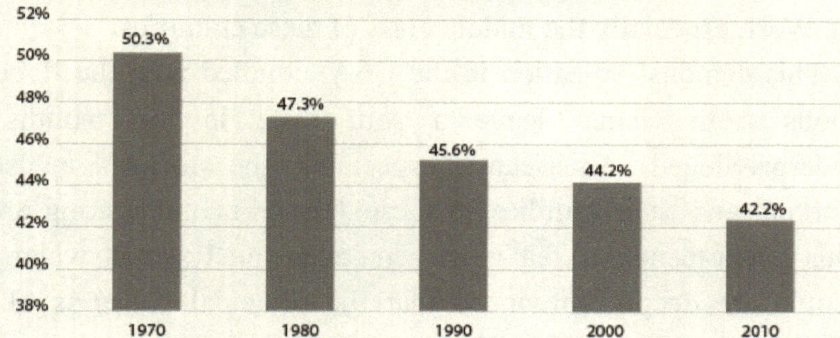

Fewer households are earning middle-class incomes

Not only have middle-class incomes stagnated, but the share of households that are earning middle-class incomes has also been in decline since the 1970s. The share of American households earning between 50 and 150 percent of the median income was 42.2 percent in 2010, down from 50.3 percent in 1970.

Percent of households with annual incomes within 50 percent of the median

Source: Alan Krueger, "The Rise and Consequences of Inequality," Speech at Center for American Progress, Washington, D.C., January 12, 2012.

Center for American Progress

The decline in Household Income in the USA over the years, even during the periods of slow and rapid growths in GDP, illustrates this decline of the middle class.

It is not only the states of the Rustbelt that are hurting from the effects of a disappearing middle class, a tragedy that many pundits blame on the path of globalization begun under the presidency of Bill Clinton in the 1990s, which is characterized by a series of trade agreements that he promoted, which ushered in a new era of international trade and investment, aided by information technology, in a process of interaction and integration among the peoples, companies and governments of the trading countries of the world.

December 8, 1993, is remembered as the day Bill Clinton, the then President of the United States of America with hardly even two years of experience in office, ratified the NAFTA (North American Free Trade Agreement—an agreement signed by the USA, Canada and Mexico, creating a trilateral trade bloc in the North American continent) bill, and then stated that "NAFTA means jobs, American jobs, and good-paying American jobs."

NAFTA went into effect on January 1, 1994, and many of its opponents and even sceptics at the time are apt to say that America's manufacturing workforce started shrinking in 1994 as Mexico and Canada became more lucrative places for American manufacturers to cut cost by setting up bases there, producing cheaply, and then shipping the products back to the USA.

However, it is the January 1, 1995 transformation of GATT (General Agreement on Trade and Tariffs—a multilateral agreement regulating international trade that was born on January 1, 1948 with objectives among others to reduce tariffs and other trade barriers among trading nations, and to eliminate preferences on a reciprocal and mutually advantageous basis) into the WTO (World Trade Organization—an intergovernmental organization created for the regulation of trade between the participating countries through the provision of a framework for negotiating trade agreements, and a dispute resolution process aimed at enforcing member countries' adherence to WTO agreements) that changed the nature of the relationship between manufacturing in the USA and the globalization drive spearheaded by those with the capital and technology.

The creation of the World Trade Organization made it very easy for American corporations, especially its manufacturing companies, to carry out a far more extensive expansion into China's opening and rapidly growing market which has even proven to be far more profitable than it was anticipated three decades ago. And these American business entities were not wrong. But they made those profits at the price of losing their long-term competitive advantages to other foreign enterprises. The globalization drive is bringing India, Indonesia, Vietnam, Thailand and a host of other countries into the fold of manufacturing nations, thereby increasing the need for America's industrial workers to improve their skills and focus on high-end manufacturing jobs that are the future of American manufacturing if the country must have an edge over the rising number of cheaper manufacturing nations of the world.

Median incomes of the middle class and other tiers fell from 1999 to 2014

Median income of households, by income tier, in 2013-14 dollars and scaled to reflect a three-person household

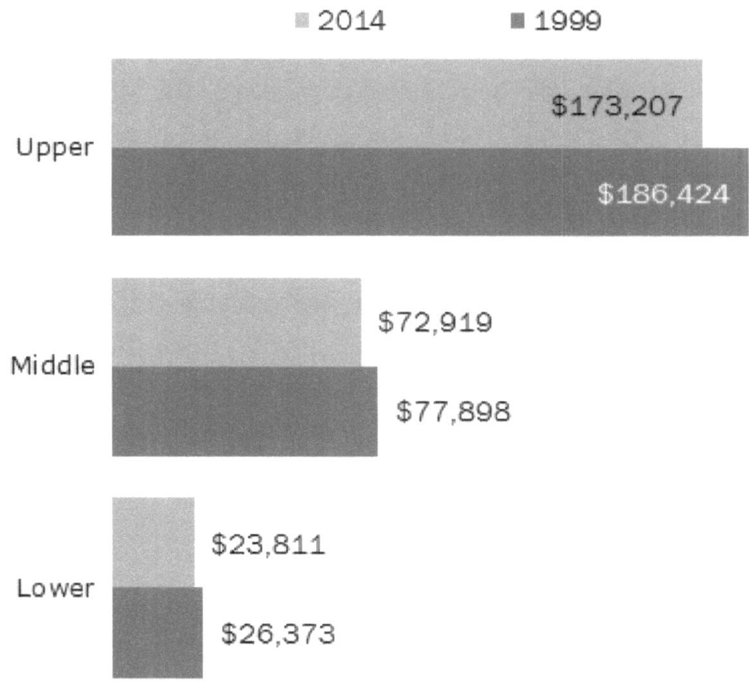

Note: The income data collected in the 2000 decennial census were for calendar year 1999.

Source: Pew Research Center analysis of the 2000 decennial census and 2014 American Community Survey (IPUMS)

"America's Shrinking Middle Class: A Close Look at Changes Within Metropolitan Areas"

PEW RESEARCH CENTER

In the USA, advocates of Free Trade and Globalization are apt to say that fair trade among free markets does more than simply enrich America; that it encourages investment and growth; that it enriches all business parties and countries that carry out transactions with one another; that it raises a worldwide demand for American products; that it increases understanding between the different peoples and the different countries of the world; that it helps dispel long-held hatreds; and that it lifts people out of poverty and ignorance. In fact they are apt to peddle the benefits of fair trade as reasons why they supported the building of free-market institutions in Eastern Europe, in Russia and the former Soviet republics, and in other former Marxist states of the world such as Ethiopia, Vietnam, Angola, Cambodia, Cuba; they are apt to use fair trade as a justification for their support of commercial liberalization in China, which is the world's fastest-growing market today, basing their argument on the postulation that democracy helps make the world safe for commerce, just as commerce helps make the world safe for democracy.

The free trade idea was a US-led Western effort to control manufacturing in China, but it apparently backfired as the Chinese copied most of the technologies the foreign entities transferred to their country, and then went about creating rival manufacturers of their own that besides competing with the rest of the world on legal terms, are equally competing with the Western-owned companies in China, the rest of the world and even in the Western countries. Anti-globalists that have a beef with China's trade practices accuse it of flooding every country in the world with cheap Chinese products as well as with fake Western-copyrighted products.

Damage Imports do to US. Industrial Production

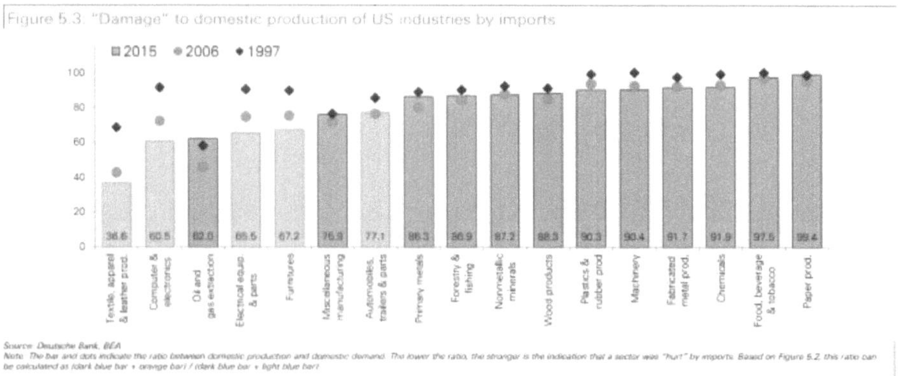

The ripple effect of these developments is lost opportunities for the millions of American who make a living from their strong elbows by churning out goods in America's factories. To find out the reasons for the lost opportunities, we would have to answer these unavoidable questions:

- Who is to be blamed for this growing problem?
- When did it all start?

The average American worker, and more especially America's middle class that is reeling from the negative results of globalization, fails to understand that the process of American export of jobs to countries where the cost of labor is cheap began in the 1980s under the leadership of Ronald Reagan, a Republican president who is today the icon of the Republican Party. It is true Bill Clinton sealed the deal of whatever had been brewing by leading the world in creating NAFTA and WTO. Irrespective of that, it is under the administrations of George W. Bush and Barack Obama that globalization attained its height. So:

Did Bill Clinton truly believe NAFTA and WTO would create more jobs and bring greater prosperity to America?

- Was the 42nd president of the United States of America convinced that the internet would be the greatest instrument to end poverty?

Most pundits would say that his advisers, the leading corporations in America, the media and the financial institutions gave him no reason to think that globalization would not be great for America. So, even if his presidency brought greater economic prosperity to America, the average American blames him for the negative effects that NAFTA and WTO are having on the wellbeing of the American middle-class today.

It is also true the Democratic Party under Bill Clinton started moving from the left to the center around the time that NAFTA and WTO were created. However, worthy of particular note is the fact that since he started moving away from what has traditionally been the base of the Democratic Party for decades (the working class made up mostly of White Americans who for generations have been involved with manufacturing, trade unions etc.), the party has never stopped tilting towards the center of American politics. It is understandable then why the victims of this transfer of jobs abroad and of America's deindustrialization associate Bill Clinton's presidency and faith in globalization with the loss of American manufacturing prowess, a decline that is the cornerstone of their economic plight today.

By moving the Democratic Party to the center, Bill Clinton made the party of Franklin Delano Roosevelt become a party of the professional class. And in a process that had been ongoing since the 1990s, the uneducated and the less educated of the working class have been shifting more and more to the right of American politics, and by default to the Republican Party. And strange as it may sound, what we have today is a switch of poles. In fact, politics in America has been transformed to the point where the elites are the only ones who still believe that the Republican Party stands for less government, big businesses and the rich; and that the Democratic Party stands for the working class etc.

Globalization during the recent decades has produced tectonic movements beneath the surface not only of American politics, but also of the politics of other countries of the world that became major partners with one another in the globalization drive led by the United States of America. And it is not only in America that the gains of this globalization have been going to the top instead of to everybody, which was the stated intention for the creation of NAFTA and WTO in the first place. While globalization swelled the ranks of the middle class in the rest of the world, especially China, it not only shrank the ranks of the middle class in the USA, it also increased the ranks of the lower class.

The deindustrialization or transfer of jobs abroad affected the different states of the union in varying ways. But the one thing these different states share in common is the fact that globalization resulted in industries with low domestic production to demand ratios, due to the profitability of imports. In fact, in 2015, imports adversely affected three distinct categories of industries in the USA:

(i) Those industries that had suffered a major drop in domestic production to domestic demand ratio over a short period. These were mostly the furniture, computer and electronics, and electrical equipment and parts. The USA's domestic production of computer and electronics met only 61% of the demand in 2015, down from 92 percent in 1997.

(ii)   Industries that experienced their drop in domestic production to demand ratio prior to 2006 due mainly to imports. These are mostly the 'automobiles, trailers and parts' and the 'textile, apparel and products' industries. In the case of the textile industry, domestic production met only 36.6% of domestic demand in 2015, down from more than 80% in the 1980s.

(iii)   Industries such as 'oil and gas extraction' and other categories of manufacturing with low domestic production to demand ratios, but that had actually been growing or are stable now compared to the past years and decades. Texas and the north-central states are the most affected in this category.

A deeper pry into the above results reveals that most of the states that have been negatively affected are the Rustbelt states. It is they who lost most of the high-end jobs in automobiles, computer, and electronics, trailers, and parts, industries that are likely to be automated in the near future, but that would make the most impact if fully revived.

The Democratic presidential candidate Hillary Clinton apparently failed to learn some useful lessons from the effects of globalization and the shift of the Democratic elites to the center, which the castrated ranks of manufacturing workers hold her husband and former president Bill Clinton responsible for. What these workers found even stranger was the fact that the political establishment's Democratic elites tend to focus more on the urban areas that were the major beneficiaries of globalization. In fact, politicians of the Democratic Party are inclined to pay little attention to the rural areas that globalization wrecked so badly.

The upper echelons of the Democratic Party ignored the poverty-stricken parts of America during the election like they did in other elections in the past, even though they found it fashionable to appear in poverty-stricken and disaster-struck parts of the world as a show of empathy, leaving many to wonder whether their actions were not directed at the media.

Over the years, even the Clintons have been accused of focusing their attention on Africa, the inner cities of America's urban centers, and Haiti as areas left behind, when the Rustbelt that Bill Clinton's presidency set up for disaster in the long run, should have been the area for Hillary Clinton to focus her campaigns on.

Thus, the populous white working class that had been moving to the right since the 1990s felt left out. That along with the other factors explain why the Rustbelt states of Wisconsin, Pennsylvania, Michigan, and Ohio that usually voted for candidates of the Democratic Party in the past presidential elections, switched their support to Donald Trump in the 2016 race for the White House either by voting for him, by voting for third party candidates or by abstaining altogether.

It is very likely that Donald Trump would follow through some aspects of his deglobalization promises in the long run, and we should expect to see him lead America into some sort of a trade war with China. He has been accusing the Asian giant not only of unfair trade practices, but also of manipulating its currency the yuan in order to increase its exports. However, it is highly unlikely that Donald Trump would take the USA out of the Trans-Pacific Partnership trade deal.

CHAPTER EIGHT

Dissatisfaction with the Choice of Candidates

When compared to the 2012 Presidential Election which gave voters a choice of seven candidates, but where the third-party candidates were so insignificant that they pulled only 1.9million votes (1.53%) between the five of them, we see that voter apathy was more widespread in the 2016 race for the White House than was the case in 2012 or 2008. In fact, pundits, the faces of the media and scholars all agree that the number of people who elected not to vote for nominees of either the Republican or Democratic parties increased to 4.5 million votes, nearly tripling the 2012 count.

Votes for Third Party/Other (millions)

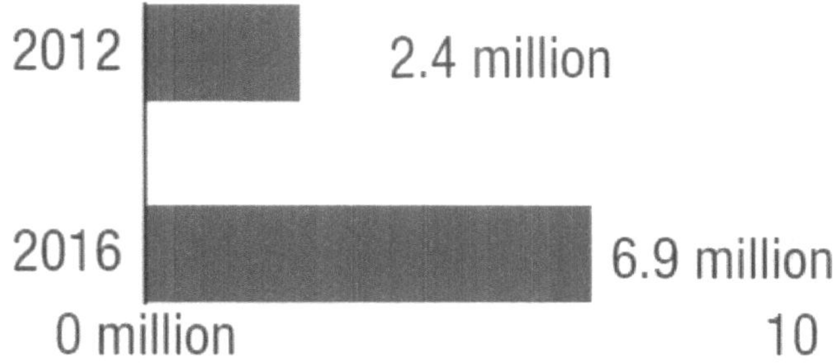

Votes for third party or candidates outside the major parties in 2012 vs. 2016.

It's difficult to say precisely which of the two major-party candidates these voters would have leaned towards. Libertarian Gary Johnson got more than 4 million votes (or 3 percent), up from 1.3 million in 2012. Green Party candidate Jill Stein got 1.3 million votes in this election, only about 1 percent overall. But one thing for sure is the fact that more young voters chose third-party candidates in the 2016 election. In fact, the number of young voters between the ages of 18-29 years remained the same as in 2012. The major difference in 2016 is that more of these young voters voted for third party/others than in the previous election.

Third Party/Other % Vote for the 18-29 age group:

Presidential Election	Third Party/Other Vote (%)
2012	3
2016	8

CHAPTER NINE

Clearness of the Message and Campaign Slogans

In one of his standup comedy shows, South African comedian Trevor Noah pointed out something peculiar about American commentators that hardly anyone can dispute—be it in sports, political or other disciplines. He said that American commentators, anchormen, and anchorwomen elaborate a lot and come up with too many statistics about the players that he finds baffling. This phenomenon also translates into the political arena. American politicians have been too detailed-oriented during their campaigns when the average voter's attention span is understandably short. Voters want short simple answers to the problems afflicting the country, succinct statements that are fact-based, that's all. In fact, the American electorate wants even more concise plans on ways to improve their lives. And one thing most politicians don't seem to have realized is the fact that voters now understand there exist more untruths than truths beneath the factual explanations and promises politicians make these days. So, the trust factor comes into play here more than the elaborate promises. Donald Trump did an effective job of tapping the trust factor and it reflected itself where it mattered the those—Midwestern America. They bought his simple messages big time.

Donald Trump's simple slogan of "Make America Great Again" (MAGA) said a thousand things that Hillary Clinton's elaborate speeches and promises could not. In fact, the short and striking phrase cast him in the eyes of voters as someone with the ability to do a far better job of turning things around and making America stronger, richer and more secure than his Democratic Party rival. In fact, 82% of Americans viewed him on election day as someone who "Can bring the needed change" as compared to 14% for Hillary Clinton. MAGA made that difference. This contrasts with the 90% who thought Hillary Clinton "Has the right experience", compared to Donald Trump's 7%. When it came to the person who cared about the welfare of the average American more than the other, Hillary Clinton came on top of her Republican rival by 57% to 34%. 65% of the voters thought the Democratic Party candidate "Has a good judgment" compared to Donald Trump, who scored 25% among those polled in October 2016.

Future political campaigns would have to do a better job of reading the mood of voters and of addressing their hopes, dreams, and expectations accordingly. Voters demanding fundamental changes would need to be addressed with pointed plans wrapped around short slogans. These short slogans like Donald Trump's "Make America Great Again", Vladimir Lenin's "Peace, Bread and Land", and Barack Obama's "Change We Can Believe In" and the chant "Yes We Can", show the effectiveness of simple words and catchy phrases that voters do not need to rack their brains to remember.

CHAPTER TEN

Turnout

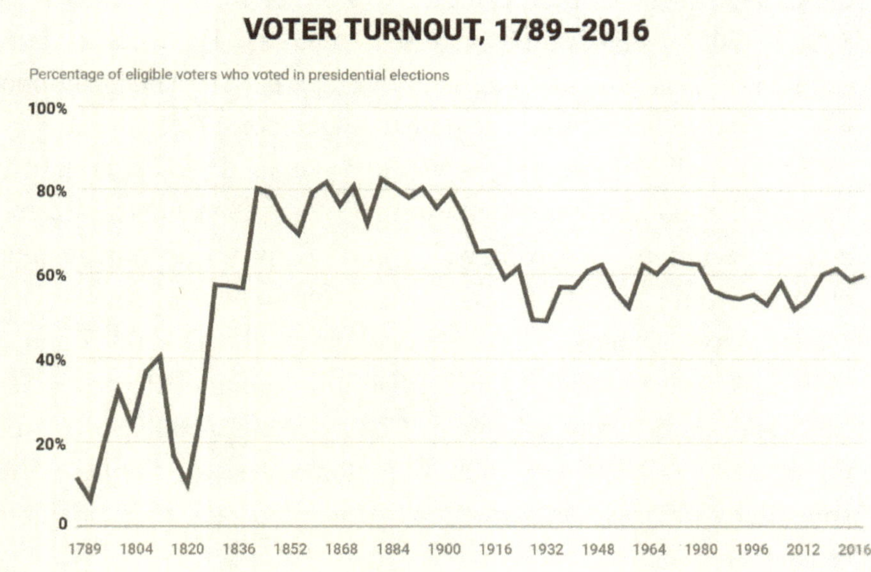

It is not surprising that voter turnout in the 2016 Presidential Election was higher than in 2012. It all started right in the primaries. Bernie Sanders and Donald Trump galvanized people who had either opted out of the voting process altogether or were not planning to vote in the 2016 Presidential Election. These were people who back in early 2015, thought the race was going to be between Hillary Clinton and another mainstream politician from the Republican Party, and so convinced themselves that it would be nothing but another electoral charade. Had it been the case of two candidates that were well known in the political arena facing off against one another, candidates from the mainstream political parties, then it would have been a familiar script from the playbook of the political establishment, or a simple vetting process to get the establishment-approved person that most Americans prefer to lead the country in maintaining a system that so many US. citizens thought needed some fixing or overhaul.

Bernie Sanders and Donald Trump, two outsiders of the establishment and critics of the system's inner workings, came into the primaries promising to change things. Bernie Sanders called it a rigged system that caters to the rich and famous, promised to cleanse it, and then went around the country summoning support that came mostly from enthusiastic young Americans who had given up on the American system. He ran a left-wing campaign that was funded entirely by the common folk of America, a campaign that rejected "Corporate Finance" and that treated the media with an indifference that was interesting indeed. Yet he won the wide support of the people, to the point where he almost created an upset against Hillary Clinton in the Democratic primaries. He lost all right, but his supporters claim the Democratic Party machinery—DNC (Democratic National Committee) rigged the primaries, thereby depriving him of victory in favor of Hillary Clinton.

The Sanders-Clinton primaries involved more Democratic Party voters than any other primaries in the history of the United States of America. The winner was expected to tap this huge enthusiasm among supporters of the Democratic Party and blaze through the election into the White House, many Democrats reasoned. But that was not the case. Even though Bernie Sanders pledged his support to Hillary Clinton, even though he campaigned for her, a substantial number of his supporters failed to heed his call to back the Democratic Party nominee. In short, not all of his supporters voted for Hillary Clinton.

All the same, most of them did. But it was not enough. Why?

- On the contrary, Donald Trump did a better job of transferring all his gains in the primaries to the election itself on November 08, 2016 than Sanders-supported Hillary Clinton.

It is rational to say that Donald Trump did a brilliant job of bringing new faces into the Republican Party, mostly White Americans who had given up on the democratic process. It is true a sizable portion of the new faces he brought into the party harbor extreme right-wing views, if not ideas, but the truth of the matter is that most of the new supporters of the Republican Party harbor mainstream ideas. In fact, these new faces are mostly people of the Rustbelt who were battered by the waves of deindustrialization that hit the region over the past three decades, and the effects of the millions of jobs that got transferred from there to other countries abroad, mostly to China and Mexico. But then, Donald Trump also did a wonderful job of closing the ranks in the Republican Party, so that what until election day looked like a feud involving him and most of the Republican Party's top brass, failed to trickle down and affect the rank and file of the party who stood by him, streamed out of their homes and workplaces on November 08, 2016, and voted him to power in their numbers, so that what many pundits, newspersons, scholars and pollsters thought would be an uninspiring election ended up being one of historic proportions.

With a 55.3% voter turnout, the 2016 Presidential Election surpassed the 2012 race for the White House between Barack Obama and Mitt Romney which had a 54.9% turnout rate. And while this increase was up nationwide by 0.4%, it was higher in most of the Rustbelt states. Overall, 19 states experienced lower turnout rates compared with 2012, defying presidential-year voting that tends to increase on each cycle that an incumbent is not participating in the Presidential Election. Of particular note are Wisconsin and Ohio, where a 3% and a 4% drop respectively in turnout rate compared with 2012 revealed upon analysis that it was mostly Democratic Voters who stayed away from the polling stations. And of course, these were mostly voters who cast their ballots for Barack Obama in the 2008 and 2012 Presidential Elections.

This upswing in voter turnout hid a fundamental fact that explains why Hillary Clinton lost the election. The Democratic base failed to turn out and vote for Hillary Clinton as it did for Obama in 2008 and 2012. It is the combination of these sour-Democrats and the additional liberal Americans who decided not to vote who ended up handing the election to the maverick Donald Trump.

In a nutshell, while Hillary Clinton got 65,844,610 votes in 2016, compared to Barack Obama's 65,915,795 votes in 2012, it registered as a decline in the participation of Democratic voters in this election. The traditional Democratic base of urban Americans, minorities, and more educated voters, found Hillary Clinton less attractive, and so failed to turn out in their numbers to vote for her.

How uninspiring she was as the Democratic nominee, it is difficult to tell. But there are pundits out there who are convinced she failed to ride the very high anti-Trump sentiment among voters, something any other Democratic candidate would have taken advantage of to win the 2016 Presidential Election. Meanwhile, Donald Trump moved up instead, getting 62,979,636 votes compared to the 2012 Republican nominee Mitt Romney's 60,933,504 votes.

A big lesson to be learnt from the turnout in the 2016 race for the White House is the fact that the United States of America has a huge reservoir of potential voters, a reservoir that can be tapped by savvy politicians and revolutionaries who voice intentions to address the issues affecting those Americans of voting age who opted out of the country's electoral process because they thought the political establishment had lost touch with people like them. For that to happen, the mainstream political parties would have to move further to the right and to the left, and the third-party candidates and their political organizations would need to broaden their agendas and political manifestos to cater for these niche voters.

CHAPTER ELEVEN

Rural voters

Population Per SQ Mile (2010)

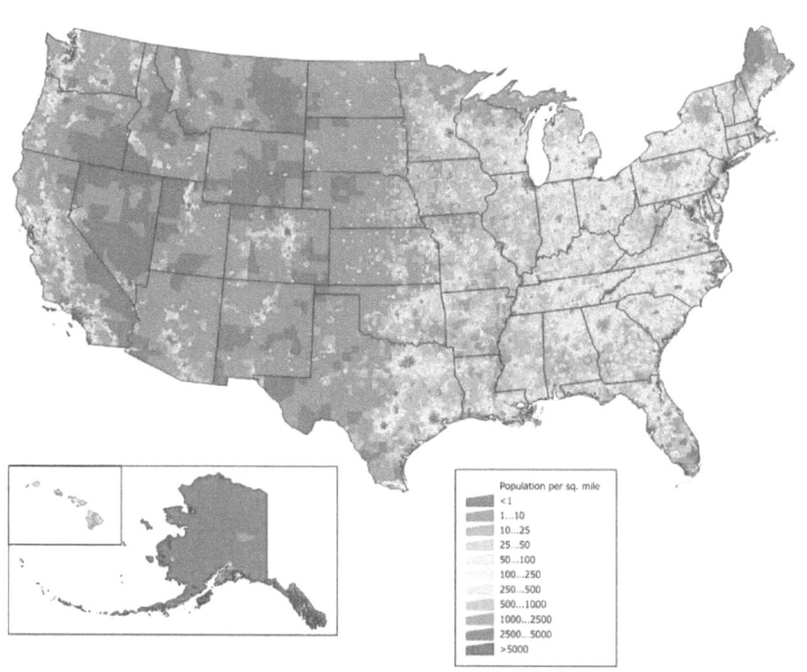

Many of those highly cognizant of the workings of the system are convinced that the Electoral College process does not create the incentives for a broad national campaign that seriously takes the rural areas into account. In fact, it does just the opposite.

The fact that Hillary Clinton lost rural America 3 to 1 to Donald Trump says a lot about the lackluster attitude of the Democratic campaign towards rural voters in the 2016 Presidential Election. Rural males are often macho and even most rural females tend to give a nod to the concept of a "Male-Dominated World". Most pundits are in agreement when it comes to the controversial view that rural America still retains much of the traditional American values of the last century. Concepts or beliefs like gay rights, minority rights, atheism, restriction of gun rights etc., that are associated with liberalism and the Democratic Left are not widely shared in the small towns, villages, and homesteads of America. In fact, they are regarded as anathema in some of these parts of the American countryside.

The Clinton campaign should have anticipated pushbacks from rural voters regarding the progress made in the areas of gay rights, abortion, and other advances that liberals and even some moderate Americans consider sacrosanct to the rights of modern man during the past eight years of the Obama presidency, advances that Hillary Clinton shared and even promised to enhance. The realization of these social rights coupled with the fact that the rural areas have been the slowest in recovering from the recent recession and the decades-old malaise that the lower and middle classes are facing, should have set off some alarm bells among Democrats. After all, recent Democratic presidential candidates lost the rural vote to Republicans by 2 to 1.

Changes in Urban/Rural Voting pattern from 2012-2016

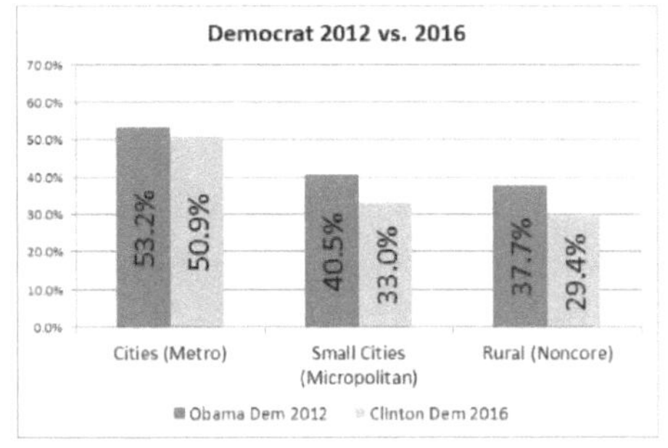

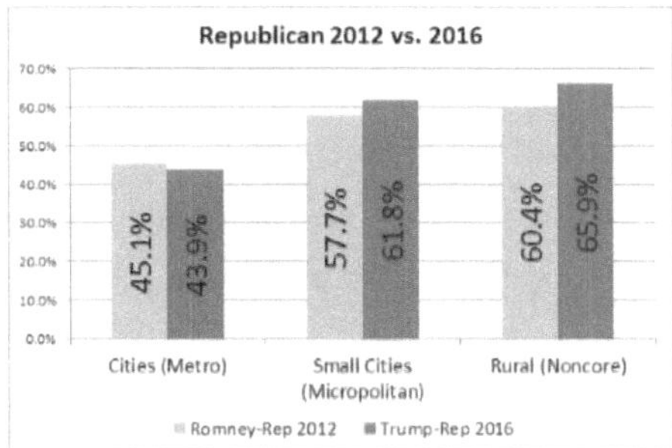

% of 2012 Electorate	Names	Obama '12	Romney '12	Clinton	Trump
22%	Big Cities	65%	34%	62%	30%
22%	Urban Suburbs	57%	41%	57%	32%
18%	The Sprawl	43%	55%	34%	55%
13%	Rural America	42%	56%	27%	64%
10%	Books and Barracks	48%	50%	39%	45%
8%	Minority Centers	51%	48%	47%	45%
7%	Faith Driven America	31%	68%	31%	52%

Some people would ask:

- Why then did Donald Trump perform so well among rural voters when he never presented any rural policy plan?

The President-elect did not present a rural plan all right, but he did a great job tapping the long-simmering anger these rural voters had against the establishment for the unfavorable trade deals struck over the years, for the constraining actions of the Environmental Protection Agency, and for what some of them perceived as a "War on American Farmers." The turnout among these voters of economically depressed communities that were still seething from the feeling of having been dismissed by Washington and the country's urban elites ended up exceeding the expectations of the Trump campaign. In fact, the high support from rural America would have presented Donald Trump with a higher margin in the Electoral vote as well as the popular vote had the rural voting bloc not shrunk dramatically over the years, owing to the fact that farms have become more efficient and many rural jobs have migrated to cities and suburbs, to the point where less than 60 million Americans or about 20% of the population live in the countryside today.

The fact that the rural population is the fastest aging also explains why rural voters made up only 17 percent of the electorate in the 2016 election. Yet, this shrinking population that's reliably Republican and which the Clinton campaign thought it really didn't need, had an outsized impact in contributing to Donald's Trump's sweep of crucial Rustbelt swing states, where among other things, turnout in suburban and urban America was lackluster for Hillary Clinton.

The Clinton campaign may have had some good reasons to think that it didn't really need rural voters, a shrinking population that is reliably Republican. Unlike the 2008 and 2012 Obama campaigns, the Clinton campaign not only failed to name a rural council, it also fell short of coming up with a robust rural-dedicated campaign infrastructure. Yet it had elaborate plans for rural America. That is why when the results trickled in on election day, the Clinton team that had what was on paper clear policy plans, found out that it had lost to a Trump campaign that made it a point of making stops in small towns where they appealed to these common folk "culturally". Besides, these rural voters never forgave Hillary Clinton for referring to most of them as "Deplorables".

It is likely that future Presidential Elections would see the candidates paying more attention to rural and suburban America, especially in the swing states where they would have to campaign the hardest. Candidates of the Democratic party, in particular, are most likely going to reduce their level of focus in urban areas where most voters live and that traditionally voted Democratic, as exemplified by the case of Pennsylvania, where 72 percent of campaign visits by Clinton and Trump in the final two months of their campaigns were to the Philadelphia and Pittsburgh areas, areas that always voted for the Democratic Party anyway. It was the same situation in Michigan, where the eight times the Clinton and Trump campaigns visited the state in the final two months of their campaigns, they went to the Detroit and Grand Rapids areas. Neither the Republican candidate nor his Democratic rival graced rural Michigan with their presence during those campaign visits.

Most experts agree today that had the Clinton campaign given more time and energy to suburban and rural America, it would not have lost the election. This is a lesson that would not be lost to future Democratic Party campaigns.

CHAPTER TWELVE

The Size of the Campaign Area

America has a unique democracy. It is only in the USA that you will find a system which favors the Electoral College over the popular vote. As a matter of fact, the electoral construct has created a situation where presidential candidates spend virtually all their campaign time in cities in 10 or 12 states instead of in 30, 40 or 50 states as most people would expect.

The 2016 presidential race was not different from previous ones when it came to the nature of the campaign events, which is defined as public events such as rallies, speeches, fairs, town hall meetings etc., during which a candidate solicits the state's voters. This count of "campaign events" excludes visits to a state for the sole purpose of conducting a private fund-raising event, of participating in a presidential debate or media interviews, of giving a speech to an organization's national convention, or of attending a non-campaign event such as the Al Smith Dinner in New York City etc.

In fact, there were 399 campaign events in the 2016 race for the White House, two-thirds (273) of which took place in just 6 states (Florida, Michigan, North Carolina, Pennsylvania, Ohio, and Virginia).

A further 94% (375) of these campaign events occurred in 12 states, 11 of which were identified as "battleground" states earlier in the year. The addition to the six states listed above included Arizona, Colorado, New Hampshire, Nevada, Iowa, and Wisconsin. So, the fact that Hillary Clinton won the popular vote and lost the election because Donald Trump won most of the electoral votes highlights the crucial importance of these battleground states. In fact, when Donald Trump tweeted on December 09, 2016 that "Campaigning to win the Electoral College is much more difficult and sophisticated than the popular vote. Hillary focused on the wrong states!", there was a lot of truth in his statement.

The other 6% of campaign events went to 14 additional states that hosted 1, 2, or 3 events. Eleven of these states (California, Connecticut, Georgia, Indiana, Minnesota, Mississippi, Missouri, New Mexico, Texas, Utah, and Washington) were visited by the Republican campaign team 22 times, but hardly saw a Democratic visit. Both campaigns visited two of these states (Maine and Nebraska) because the states award some of their Electoral votes by congressional district.

As explained further by the map below, the campaign area was not large enough and the focus of the campaign did not sufficiently tap the changing dynamics of America and American society, even though there was an expansion in the scope of the 2016 election campaigns vis-à-vis previous presidential elections.

States that had campaign events

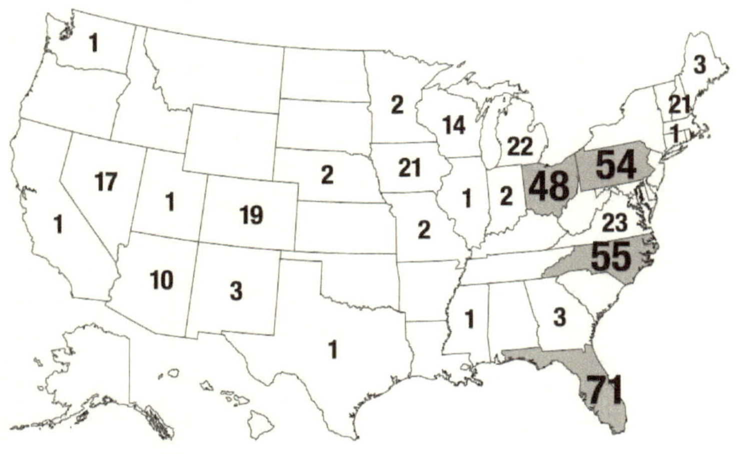

It is easy to deduce from the map above that the post-convention campaign events organized by the major-party presidential and vice-presidential nominees (Donald Trump, Mike Pence, Hillary Clinton, and Tim Kaine) were not as widespread as many people thought. Further data from the 2016 campaign indicates that 53 percent of campaign events for Donald Trump, Hillary Clinton, Mike Pence and Tim Kaine in the two months before the November election, took place in only four states (Florida, Pennsylvania, North Carolina and Ohio). During those last two months, 87 percent of campaign visits by the four candidates were in 12 battleground states, and none of the four candidates ever went to 27 states, which includes almost all of rural America.

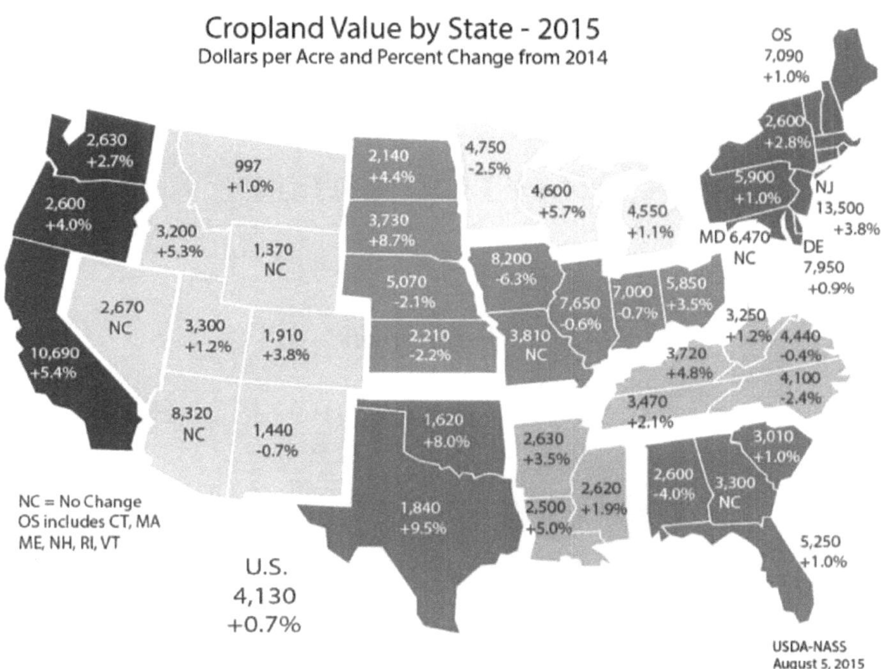

Cropland Value by State - 2015
Dollars per Acre and Percent Change from 2014
OS
7,090
+1.0%
2,630
+2.7%
997
+1.0%
2,140
+4.4%
4,750
-2.5%
4,600
+5.7%
4,550
+1.1%
2,600
+2.8%
2,600
+4.0%
3,200
+5.3%
1,370
NC
3,730
+8.7%
8,200
-6.3%
5,900
+1.0%
NJ
13,500
+3.8%
MD 6,470
NC
DE
7,950
+0.9%
2,670
NC
3,300
+1.2%
1,910
+3.8%
5,070
-2.1%
7,650
-0.6%
7,000
-0.7%
5,850
+3.5%
3,250
+1.2%
4,440
-0.4%
10,690
+5.4%
2,210
-2.2%
3,810
NC
3,720
+4.8%
4,100
-2.4%
8,320
NC
1,440
-0.7%
1,620
+8.0%
3,470
+2.1%
3,010
+1.0%
2,630
+3.5%
NC = No Change
OS includes CT, MA
ME, NH, RI, VT
1,840
+9.5%
2,500
+5.0%
2,620
+1.9%
2,600
-4.0%
3,300
NC
U.S.
4,130
+0.7%
5,250
+1.0%
USDA-NASS
August 5, 2015

CHAPTER THIRTEEN

Education

The Educational Attainment of the Voters

Demographic	Sex		Educational attainment			
	Male	Female	High school or less	Some College	College graduate	Postgraduate
Trump	53%	41%	51%	52%	45%	37%
Clinton	42%	54%	45%	43%	49%	58%

States with a lower level of education of the population and that are known to have an average IQ that is lower in comparison to other states are where Donald Trump did very well on November 08, 2016.and their propensity to back programs, promises or policies whose benefits cannot be clearly substantiated.

States and their Percentage of 25 years old with Bachelor's Degree or Higher in 2009.

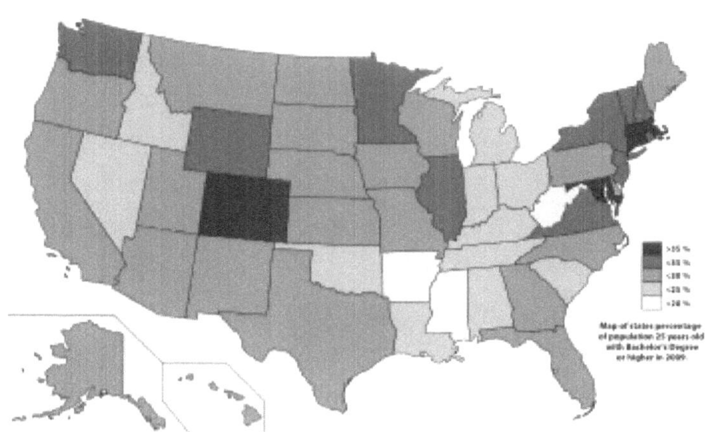

States and their percentage of 25 years old with Advanced Degree in 2009.

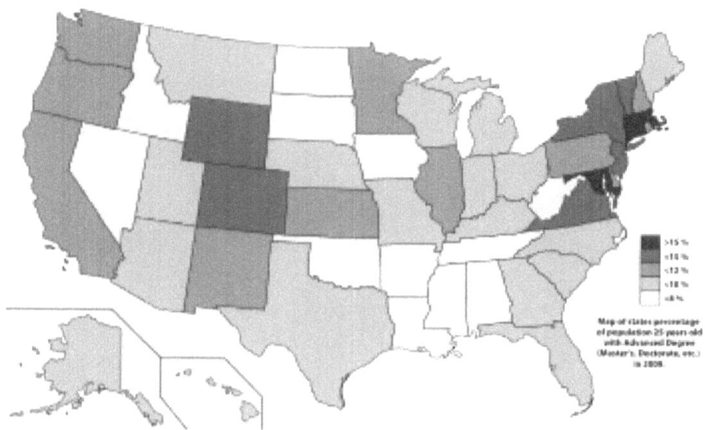

A school of thought holds that the educational level of the population mirrors the degree of political awareness or ignorance of the people. As it turned out to be, states with lower IQs also ended up having high percentages of underprivileged White Americans and disadvantaged minorities at the lower rungs of America's social and economic ladder, especially blacks. This category of White and Black Americans, most of whom are inclined to vote Republican, voted for Donald Trump. Meanwhile, most African Americans went to the polls with less enthusiasm for Hillary Clinton than they had for Barack Obama four years ago. They voted for Hillary Clinton all right, but their lower turnout failed to neutralize the support that Asians and Hispanics gave to the Republican candidate, which was higher in 2016 than in 2012.

Hillary Clinton was definitely thinking about the low level of education and low IQ of some of the people supporting Donald Trump when she described her billionaire rival's supporters during the campaigns as "Deplorables". Of course, it backfired as those who thought she addressed that adjective at them mounted a robust mobilization against her, especially in the Rustbelt. The maps above and the information below provide more insight into the level of education of the population and voters' choice in the 2016 Presidential Election

The Educational Level of the Different States

State	% High School Graduate	Rank	% Bachelor's Degree	Rank	% Advanced Degree	Rank
Wyoming	91.8%	1	23.8%	40	7.9%	38
Minnesota	91.7%	2	31.5%	10	10.3%	17
Alaska	91.4%	3	26.6%	24	9.0%	27
New Hampshire	91.3%	5	32.0%	9	11.2%	12
Vermont	91.0%	6	33.1%	7	13.3%	6
Montana	90.8%	7	27.4%	21	8.3%	36
Iowa	91.4%	3	25.1%	34	7.4%	43
Hawaii	90.4%	8	29.6%	15	9.9%	20
Utah	90.4%	8	28.5%	19	9.1%	26

State	% High School Graduate	Rank	% Bachelor's Degree	Rank	% Advanced Degree	Rank
Maine	90.2%	10	26.9%	23	9.6%	22
North Dakota	90.1%	11	25.8%	27	6.7%	48
South Dakota	89.9%	12	25.1%	34	7.3%	45
Nebraska	89.8%	13	27.4%	21	8.8%	29
Wisconsin	89.8%	13	25.7%	28	8.4%	34
Kansas	89.7%	15	29.5%	16	10.2%	18
Washington	89.7%	15	31.0%	11	11.1%	13
Colorado	89.3%	17	35.9%	3	12.7%	8
Oregon	89.1%	18	29.2%	17	10.4%	15
Massachusetts	89.0%	19	38.2%	1	16.4%	1

State	% High School Graduate	Rank	% Bachelor's Degree	Rank	% Advanced Degree	Rank
Maryland	89.0%	19	37.3%	2	16.0%	2
Connecticut	88.6%	21	35.6%	4	15.5%	3
Idaho	88.4%	22	23.9%	39	7.5%	42
Michigan	87.9%	23	24.6%	36	9.4%	24
Pennsylvania	87.9%	23	26.4%	26	10.2%	18
Ohio	87.6%	25	24.1%	38	8.8%	29
Delaware	87.4%	26	28.7%	18	11.4%	11
New Jersey	87.4%	26	34.5%	5	12.9%	7
District of Columbia	87.1%		48.5%		28.0%	
Missouri	86.8%	28	25.2%	33	9.5%	23

State	% High School Graduate	Rank	% Bachelor's Degree	Rank	% Advanced Degree	Rank
Indiana	86.6%	29	22.5%	43	8.1%	37
Virginia	86.6%	29	34.0%	6	14.1%	4
Illinois	86.4%	31	30.6%	12	11.7%	9
Oklahoma	85.6%	32	22.7%	42	7.4%	43
United States	85.3%		27.9%		10.3%	
Florida	85.3%	33	25.3%	31	9.0%	27
New York	84.7%	34	32.4%	8	14.0%	5
Rhode Island	84.7%	34	30.5%	13	11.7%	9
North Carolina	84.3%	36	26.5%	25	8.8%	29
Arizona	84.2%	37	25.6%	29	9.3%	25

State	% High School Graduate	Rank	% Bachelor's Degree	Rank	% Advanced Degree	Rank
Georgia	83.9%	38	27.5%	20	9.9%	20
Nevada	83.9%	38	21.8%	45	7.6%	41
South Carolina	83.6%	40	24.3%	37	8.4%	34
Tennessee	83.1%	41	23.0%	41	7.9%	38
New Mexico	82.8%	42	25.3%	31	10.4%	15
West Virginia	82.8%	42	17.3%	50	6.7%	48
Arkansas	82.4%	44	18.9%	49	6.1%	50
Louisiana	82.2%	45	21.4%	46	6.9%	47
Alabama	82.1%	46	22.0%	44	7.7%	40
Kentucky	81.7%	47	21.0%	47	8.5%	32

State	% High School Graduate	Rank	% Bachelor's Degree	Rank	% Advanced Degree	Rank
California	80.6%	48	29.9%	14	10.7%	14
Mississippi	80.4%	49	19.6%	48	7.1%	46
Texas	79.9%	50	25.5%	30	8.5%	32

CHAPTER FOURTEEN

The Media and the Democratic Nominee

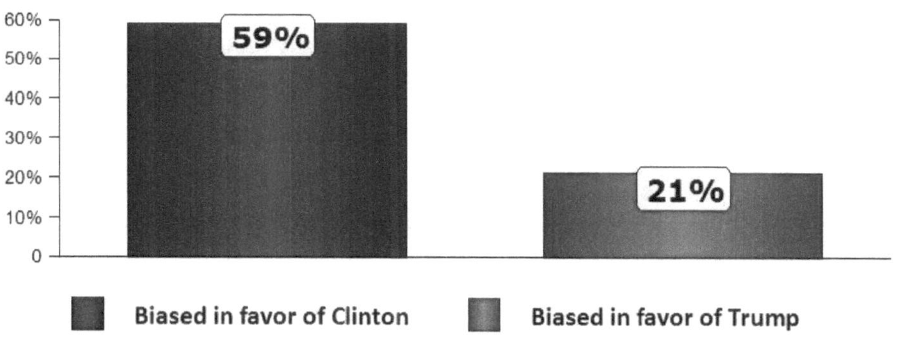

Source: Media Research Center/You Gov poll of 2,006 voters conducted Nov. 9-10. Percentages based on 1,547 voters who said "national news media coverage of the presidential campaign was biased."

Hillary Clinton emerged from the Democratic primaries a highly-publicized candidate with a questionable popularity. In fact, many Democrats, especially the young who played a pivotal role in voting Barack Obama to office in the last two Presidential Elections, showed some degree of lackluster when it came to committing themselves to the Hillary Clinton campaign. It had to take an energetic endorsement from Bernie Sanders and an open adoption of a substantial portion of his campaign platform for about half of Bernie Sanders supporters to openly embrace Hillary Clinton. A further quarter joined the Hillary Clinton bandwagon and voted for her all right, but the 10%-20% who voted for either Donald Trump or the other candidates, or who ended up not voting at all rather than casting their ballots for any of the candidates that they did not like, ended up hurting Hillary Clinton in a major way, especially in the swing states of Ohio and Florida, and in the other Rust Belt states of Michigan, Pennsylvania, and Wisconsin that the Trump campaign managed to convert into Swing States.

The mainstream media did a wonderful job of having Hillary Clinton's back, but these consent-manufacturers failed to create a Hillary Clinton that voters could regard as the modicum of the quintessential first female president of the United States of America. Something the media did a great job trying to turn around was the fact that nearly 70% of the voters thought she was untrustworthy and dishonest, far higher than the percentage that thought so of Donald Trump. So, not only did she come with a special baggage—as a controversial former first lady, as a controversial former Secretary of State vilified by the Right especially for the September 2012 Benghazi attack that was coordinated against two United States government facilities in Benghazi, Libya by members of the Islamic militant group called Ansar al-Sharia, which resulted in the deaths of the U.S. ambassador to Libya, Christopher Stevens, and three other U.S. nationals—she entered the race for the White House as a co-founder of the Clinton Foundation with her husband Hillary Clinton and her daughter Chelsea, a foundation that was recently accused of malpractices in Haiti, a foundation that could even be charged for getting unlawful donations from foreign entities. Even some Democrats expressed misgivings about her personality, citing a lack of warmth among other things as uninspiring qualities she failed to improve on.

Hillary Clinton got a lot of coverage from the mainstream media that was almost always positive, unlike her Republican rival Donald Trump who got almost the same amount of time of mainstream media coverage, though in an overwhelmingly negative light. The discrepancy in the mainstream media's coverage of the two candidates worked against Hillary Clinton in the long run because many mainstream readers and viewers smelled a rat and most of them finally came to the conclusion that there was a concerted effort to manufacture consent in the 2016 election, which they translated as a move by the establishment to take them for another ride. In fact, many of the voters in the election turned to the social media and the alternative media for news, views and guarded information that they rightfully or wrongfully thought the mainstream media tried was trying to squash or was distorting to suit an agenda.

What became obvious after election day was the fact that the demonization of Donald Trump and the almost deification of Hillary Clinton by the mainstream media worked against her in the 2016 presidential race for the White House. The American public has become wise to the media's game, some pundits say. In fact, the people are wise enough to determine which side the media is on. They have developed the ability to discount much of what is false that the media reports about the candidates in elections. Whether the mainstream media would be able to recover from the loss in its ability to influence the American public the way it did in the past is something that is difficult to tell at this early stage of its rude awakening. But one thing for sure is that the mainstream media can no longer work with just the corporatocracy in manufacturing consent. It must find common ground with alternative media outlets and the altruists of this world who have made the cause for humanity their missions in life.

The 2016 presidential election would also be remembered as

one of the most bizarre in history in the sense that it surpassed previous elections in its failure to dwell on substance, a phenomenon that the media fostered as it focused on the demonization of Donald Trump more than on real policy issues. In fact, less than twelve percent (12%) of coverage focused on the policy positions, leadership abilities or personal and professional histories of the candidates.

And to cap it all, WikiLeaks influenced the election against Hillary Clinton in the sense that it provided the leaks that embarrassed the Democratic Party and exposed the partially of the DNC (Democratic National Committee) for favoring Hillary Clinton against Bernie Sanders. Its revelation of the fact that Donna Brazile who briefly served as the interim chairperson for the Democratic National Committee provided Hillary Clinton with the questions that she later asked her in the Clinton/Trump debate, served as the single biggest embarrassment for the Democratic Party as it highlighted what some commenters called the growing dishonesty within the party leadership. No one can say whether these revelations by WikiLeaks failed or did not fail to influence the thinking of voters.